5S YOUR LIFE

Stop Procrastination and Start Self-organization

Luciana Paulise

Luciana Paulise
July 2020

ISBN: 9798667931515
Imprint: Independently published
Beaumont, Texas, USA

Dedicated to my brother
Octavio

Foreword

As soon as I sat down at the table, I immediately knew what was missing: the peanuts.

I was a process engineer at Duracell Batteries in my early twenties in LaGrange, Georgia, a manufacturing town sixty-five miles south of Atlanta. As a reward for successfully completing the past several months of training, my manager had brought the entire team to a local barbeque restaurant called Hog Heaven for lunch. The restaurant's faded red paint and sloping ceilings made you feel like you were driving up to someone's warm, countryside home. Inside, its decor of hand-carved wooden pigs and checkered tablecloths made it seem like you were being invited into the kitchen of a longtime family friend.

We were hungry. And the unshelled peanuts that customers crushed and feasted upon while perusing the menu were missing. The peanuts were always served in precipitously overfilled metal buckets that were placed in the center of each table.

The center of our table was empty.

The team had just completed the final days of a multi-week lean manufacturing training at our factory. Finding ways of producing our consumer batteries in efficient ways was the focus of all of our workshops and experiments. When running assembly lines that produced several hundred batteries per minute, each moment the line was not running meant another moment of lost productivity, another end-user whose supply of 9-Volt or AAA batteries was being limited.

As we learned, much of this wasn't caused by the complexities of chemical engineering or mechanical design, but by missing tools. A replacement pump that couldn't be assembled because the mechanic had to walk two lines over to borrow the right sized hex wrench; a production line that had to stop for forty-five minutes because they had too much of one battery ingredient and not enough of another; an operator that had the right tool in their possession, but had to dig through multiple drawers of their equipment cabinet before they could find it.

Our team's training resulted in all of us having the fundamental principles of effectiveness and efficiency driven into our thoughts. The talents and technical capabilities of our team weren't going to be very useful if the tools needed at a given moment were not the tools we had right in front of us.

The training had taught us how to see our surroundings differently, to know if what we needed was exactly what we had; to know that if one of us walked twenty feet away to another line, that the setup, the tools, and the operational processes were the exact same as the line that we had come from. Thanks to these new organizing superpowers that had been granted us, our teams could now operate any assembly line in any part of the factory, regardless of who was there or what time of day it was running.

With our newly trained eyes, we even looked at our frequently visited barbeque restaurant differently. We thought about how the menu was laid out so we could always find our favorite dishes quickly, which bottle of hot sauce on the table was the spiciest and more importantly, if a favorite hot sauce was missing. (Seconds after sitting down, our server dropped off a freshly filled bucket of peanuts, so crisis averted.) Now it was time to finally celebrate in a way that only manufacturing engineers could: we spent that lunch hour cracking peanut shells, enjoying home made sandwiches covered in hot sauce, and sharing our plans for how we intended to use that simple but futuristic tool we had been practicing for months: 5S.

Around four decades before Marie Kondo taught the world to spark joy through tidying up, Toyota had already devised a process for keeping things in order and within reach. While this practice to sort, store, shine, standardize, and self-organize soon became the heart of any efficient manufacturing operations, the usage of the methodology soon spread to organizing office spaces and any other place in our personal and professional lives that needed less disorganization and more purpose.

But 5S is not about organizing for the sake of organizing.

5S is about taking away all those minutiae of our daily routines that are inconsequential so that we can focus on those things that are most important: our relationships, our environment, those actions we take to become professionally and personally fulfilled.

Thanks to this highly tactical guide that Luciana has written, you can now learn how to take the practice of 5S into your own workplace or home. The greatest promise of this guide doesn't just rest in the organizing strategies that it will teach you. Within the world that 5S creates around us, the greatest reward is what that environment allows us to become.

Save space for the hot sauce.

Austin S. Lin
Chair, ASQ Board of Directors
asq.org

(May 2020, San Francisco, California)

Preface

The day my brother Octavio died from cancer a year ago, I decided to publish this book and dedicate it to him. He taught me the pleasure of reading. Thanks to him, I was young enough to write and had already kept an inventory of all the books I had read. He always tried to teach me the power of cleanliness and organization, but I was always "too busy" to clean up.

Cancer is a terrible disease. Hopefully, more patients are surviving it, but not all of them, despite the efforts of the best experts. Malign tumors are caused by abnormal cells that multiply uncontrollably and spread to other body parts, blocking and destroying other functions.

We tend to think that the more, the merrier, but cancer shows that is not always the case. Many companies suffer from a similar type of "disease" called procrastination. Simple tasks don't get done waiting for approvals; unneeded materials are stacked for no reason; obsolete procedures that destroy customer loyalty are followed, and team members become obstacles to others. The unnecessary grows exponentially while the total productivity decreases significantly until the company is not agile enough to survive the next crisis.

Many systems help individuals to improve productivity and self-discipline. But how many of them help entire teams to become more productive? Working with others adds complexity to any organization, even families. And there is always someone else you can blame for not getting things done or for a growing number of unneeded inventories.

Google, named one of the most innovative companies in 2019[1], launched the Aristotle project to determine what prevented teams from being successful and what made them work best. They found out that what mattered was less about who was on the team and more about how the team worked together.

To make the team successful and productive, you need group norms that help team members self-organize the space in a certain way that they can interact seamlessly in any given situation without being continuously

---

[1] https://www.forbes.com/sites/louiscolumbus/2019/03/24/the-most-innovative-companies-of-2019-according-to-bcg/#23f381a7486d

told. Self-organization is not a genetic trait. It is a way of working that can be learned and promoted. So this is where 5S will help you.

The 5S method is widely known in industrial companies around the world. Still, most of them barely use it to meet the minimum health and safety requirements, losing motivation a year later. Some consultants call it 6S or 7S. Others argue that workplace organization prevents a place from being creative.

Still, multiple case studies show that these five steps are much more than sorting and labeling. Working with hundreds of teams, I learned how 5S starts changing small individual habits that contribute to team self-organization. As a result, trailblazing organizations have uncovered how 5S can change their culture to reduce procrastination, boost productivity and employee engagement.

The 5S your Life system helps team members to become more focused, empowered and innovative every day. Especially useful during pressing times, teams will learn to improve housekeeping and safety and reduce friction and obstacles, helping them become more successful at work and in other areas of their lives.

Companies will strive not only for a physically safe but also for a psychologically safe environment where employees, customers, suppliers and even communities can thrive.

You will smooth your way to do better what you love doing.

Read the 5S steps, and practice the 15 micro-steps every day when doing simple things. For example, you will go to restaurants, clinics, auto shops and realize you complain about why they haven't used 5S yet. When this happens, you will have started self-organization. Less is more.

PART I:

Self-organization vs. procrastination

5S INTRODUCTION

"Perfection is achieved, not when there is nothing more to add, but when there is nothing left to take away" Antoine de Saint-Exupery

It's a high-demand period. Customers are lost if deliveries are not on time. The higher the pressure to finish faster, the more employees and managers cut corners.

They all stop doing things that they believe, or are told, will not increase productivity, such as sorting or cleaning—the backlog of un-sorted items increases. Items out of place and dirt increase chaos, so time is spent looking for tools for setup and repairing machines not well maintained. As a result, total production time increases in the long term, aggravating the initial problem.

Fifty shopfloor workers spend an average of 5 minutes looking for various items; the cumulative is about 250 minutes or 4,2 hours of the production workday.

There is still some time used to store, about 500 minutes per day (approximately one day of an 8-hour production shift).

When the same team implements 5S, on the 30th day of the project, the throughput is about 26.5 completed orders per day, a 10% improvement when compared to less than 24 completed orders for the current as-is. The total time spent looking for items reduces from 0.6 to about 0.2 work hours per day. This is a 67% improvement.

With the time saved in setup and repair, idle time is reduced.

With these savings, workers can have more time doing more value-adding activities, while time spent in setup and repair activities decreases.[2]

---

[2] Extracted from the implementation of 5s lean tool using system dynamics approach. Oleghe omogbaia*, konstantinos salonitisa. Manufacturing department, cranfield university, bedfordshire, england.

What is 5s

5S is a set of habits that drive individual productivity and team self-organization through a lean workplace.

Through 5 steps, sort, store, shine, standardize and self-organize, you and your team will learn what to do, how to do it and when to do it without being told.

More than a method, it implies a change in the way you work, a cultural change. It is one of the first tools recommended for a company that is trying to reduce unneeded costs, increase employee engagement, and improve quality and productivity and safety at the same time.

Even though 5S is typically implemented in manufacturing companies, it can be used in any organization, even at home.

IKEA[3] researched in Spain and discovered that almost half of Spanish people (48%) lose something at least once a week. If the average time spent looking for something is between 1 and 10 minutes, that adds up to over 6.5 months of our lives, which is equivalent to almost 5,000 hours spent looking for things.

You can now estimate how much time and money your company spends trying to find things, buy new ones, explain to the customer, blame others, or miss deadlines. And there is a cost that is not even accounted for: the cost of disengagement and frustration.

The 5 Steps

5S is based on five Japanese terms, all starting with S (the English version also starts with S), representing steps towards the final aim, team self-organization.

1) **Sort:** Separate unneeded items to increase focus on what is needed.
2) **Store:** organize all the needed items in a specific "home" to be ready to use.
3) **Shine:** Set a new level of cleanliness that enables spotting potential problems.

---

[3] https://www.ikea.com/es/en/ideas/how-much-time-do-we-spend-searching-for-things-around-the-home-pubec2a8ae0

4) **Standardize:** Engage the team to find a system to sort, store and shine.

5) **Self-organize:** Train the team to repeat the 5S steps every day until they become a habit.

5S is like a stair with five levels (see image 1). You start by sorting at the first step, and you get to the last stage to achieve self-organization and sustain it.

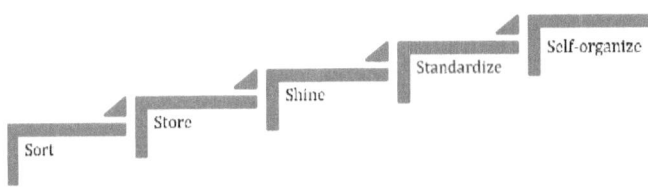

Image 1

A little story about the origins of 5S

The 5S method has its origins in Japan. It was first popularized by Taiichi Ohno, who designed the Toyota Production System and Shigeo Shingo, who also put forward the concept of poka-yoke (See chapter TOOLS TO COMPLEMENT 5S).

5S is a basic first step to implementing quality improvement, especially in Japan. And the main reason why is that the importance of organization and cleanliness is rooted in the Japanese culture. Japan itself is clean and tidy, and people are disciplined.

Public spaces, including streets, train stations and toilets, are clean without trash. It's difficult to find trash boxes on the streets because people are encouraged to take the garbage home. At school, students are supposed to clean their own classrooms as a part of school activities. On arriving at school or getting back from work, students and workers leave their shoes in lockers or at the entrance.

Japanese became so clean-conscious basically because of their hot and humid environment, which is bacteria prone, so cleanliness and respect for others directly mean good health in their culture. Invisible dirt like germs and bacteria are a source of concern. When people catch colds or flu, they already have the habit of wearing surgical masks to avoid infecting other people.

Self-organization, the skill of the future

After the COVID-19 virus outbreak in January 2020, the entire world had to change its behaviors. Everyone started being more mindful about cleanliness and respecting personal spaces. Wearing surgical masks and leaving the shoes outside the house, just like the Japanese, become a healthy habit.

Manufacturing companies had to reduce production to allow for social distancing. Hospitals and restaurants had to change the way they operated to take care of their customers and patients. Most Services, like marketing, accounting or call centers, shifted their way of working by sending employees to work from home.

As the U.S. saw a 125% increase[4] in remote work usage, companies had to start communicating differently, with team structures and leaders' roles changing.

The organizations that adapted most quickly were self-organizing teams[5]: small groups, ideally around eight but no more than twenty people, autonomous, transparent, decisive, cross-functional, and self-disciplined.

A study conducted by McKinsey[6] found that "companies that ranked higher on managing the impact of the Covid-19 crisis were also those with agile practices more deeply embedded in their enterprise operating models." Agile teams continued their work almost seamlessly, while non-agile teams struggled to be productive.

This concept was also apparent on the homefront. While my husband and I were working from home, my daughter, Sol, could still go

---

[4]   https://www.aternity.com/wp-content/uploads/2020/04/Global-Remote-Work-Productivity-Tracker-Vol-1.pdf

[5] *Sky High: How Self-Organizing Teams And A 'We' Culture Set The Stage For Innovation.* Luciana Paulise. Quality Progress Magazine March 2020.

[6]   https://www.mckinsey.com/business-functions/organization/our-insights/an-operating-model-for-the-next-normal-lessons-from-agile-organizations-in-the-crisis

to school and complete kindergarten in the last week of June. How come, I wondered, could she continue her routine amid this crisis? Sol attended a small school part of the Acton Academy, with no more than 15 students of various ages. They transitioned to studying online between April and May, but the move had been seamless. Sol already knew what she had to do and how as it was a self-paced school. While I was hearing that most schools in the world were struggling to connect students and teachers, Sol's school had done a great job in keeping the connection with the students and the job done.

Non-agile teams were pushed to become more agile, even without knowing. Many leaders were used to checking on employees at all times before the pandemic. Now, while remote, managers had to learn to trust employees to know what they were doing. Manager and workers learned:

1. To re-connect to the company's purpose and values in order to serve the customer needs better. Working at the same location made it easier to see the connection with others. Working apart, employees demand more communication. People look for their small tribe to maintain a strong human connection.

2. Workers learned to be more self-reliant and improved independent decision-making when managers were unavailable. Employees also increased attention to detail, especially in handling customer data. Information had to be shared more openly to increase trust and self-confidence. While working at the office, employees had the luxury of relying on leaders' decision-making processes. Moving remotely pushed decision-making to the front-line.

3. Respect individual needs. Previously, employees were not asked for input on how they wanted to go about their jobs. After Covid-19, employees' needs started to be taken into account. Some people were alone and were able to work more, while others lived with their kids and had to work at night to focus. At the same time, the Black Lives Matter movement intensified the need for equality, diversity and inclusion of minorities.

4. Empower themselves to become more autonomous. Employees had to define new ways to get their job done in a different setting. They had also had to learn to set new goals based on their current availability.

These four values — connection, attention, respect and empowerment — are practiced daily by self-organized teams in agile organizations. During hard times, self-organization became one of the most valuable skills in organizations to help them overcome the unexpected.

While implementing 5S solely doesn't make your company agile (it is not even considered part of the tools in the agile skill set), it prepares the team for the transition. It focuses on the most critical and challenging part of agile practices, the behaviors and culture enabling self-organization.

Self-organization is a muscle

Self-organization is not new but is not widespread either. Companies learn to dictate procedures while employees learn to follow them and avoid asking questions.

Self-organization, instead, is when team members know what to do by getting information from the environment or the other team members, not through a leader or a hierarchy. It is a process in which behavioral patterns emerge from interactions among the lower-level components of the system, the team members. Just like in biological systems such as a large group of fish, the organization is not achieved through a leader. Instead, "each fish gathers information about its nearest neighbor and responds accordingly."[7]

5S your life is to set the stage for success. It is about cultivating a mindset where you take ownership of your life, gathering cues from the environment and your teammates instead of waiting for someone to tell you what to do. You learn to observe what's out there, and that experience takes you to a never-ending loop: repeat the rules and required behaviors until they become a habit, observe your environment to detect any changes or threats, and make small changes when needed, in agreement with your team, to improve the process over time.

---

[7] Self-Organization in Biological systems. Scott Camazine, Jean-Louis Deneubourg, Nigel R. Franks, James Sneyd, Guy Theraulaz and Eric Bonabeau. Princeton University Press. 2001.

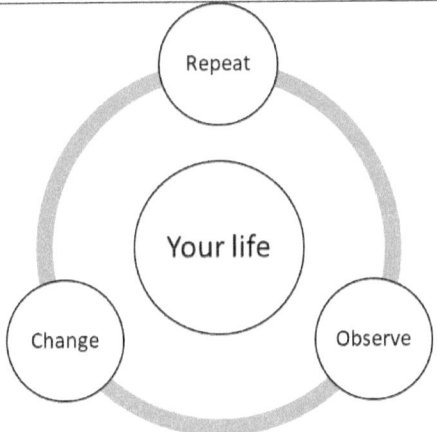

Image 2

Roy F. Baumeister explains that "Psychology has found two traits that consistently lead to success in a vast assortment of undertakings. One is intelligence. The other is self-control."[8]

Researchers have also found that you cannot increase your intelligence (not yet, at least), but you can improve your self-control. It is like a muscle.

Self-organization, just like self-control, is also a muscle that you can train.

To improve it, all you have to do is exercise it regularly by adding new habits to your routine, practicing them every day. Starting Self-organization at work, it will spill over into other areas, too, helping you get exponentially better. You will get more of what you want to accomplish done.

---

[8] https://www.highperformanceinstitute.com/blog/self-control-high-performance-and-the-limits-of-willpower

Benefits of applying 5S

The main benefit of 5S is that it helps to practice your self-organization muscle every day, with simple tiny actions or micro changes. For example, when you are sorting out a document that you don't need anymore or a shirt that you don't use, you start to self-organize and stop procrastination.

And you are not only starting new habits, but at the same time, you are building an environment that helps you sustain these new habits in the future. The labels, bins, and colors are all cues that tell you what to do and keep you focused on what is important and urgent. Employees start to understand how the workplace impacts their mood, behaviors, and success, so they learn to take care of it.

In a family, cleaning and keeping the house organized can be a one-person show, or the entire family, including the kids, can be invited to participate. When all the family members understand what it takes to keep the house clean, they all engage actively to clean and avoid getting things dirty. 5S helps the "family" self-organize and arrange items purposefully so that everyone knows what to do, how and when. Without being told.

Team members learn to remove any obstacles in the work environment to make it more:
- ✓ Organized: everything has a "home"
- ✓ Safe: problems are detected easily and removed
- ✓ Respectful: everyone does what needs to be done

Hard Benefits: What is in it for the organization?

5S has become a smart investment in multiple industries. While the costs of implementation are relatively low, the benefits of the projects are significant.
- ✓ Increased productivity levels and fewer delays, even during a turnaround
- ✓ Reduced waste on the floor and inside cabinets
- ✓ Optimized use of space
- ✓ Increased number of safety observations
- ✓ Improved detection of water, oil and product leaks
- ✓ Improved equipment maintenance
- ✓ Improved inventory management and retrieval time
- ✓ Continuous autonomous inspection

Some hard benefits reported:

33% Improved lead time[9]

68% Reduced inventory[10]

38% Reduced physical "footprint" of floor space required in an operating room for equipment, instruments, and supplies[11]

30% Reduced preparation time[12]

85% Decreased mistakes[13]

Soft Benefits: What is in it for the employees?

✓ Safe environment
✓ Clear responsibilities
✓ Relationships based on respect
✓ Empowerment to find the solutions in the frontline
✓ Joy at work
✓ A workplace to be proud of
✓ New habits applied at home too

Why would team members get involved in 5S? Because they are the ones with the most benefits in their day-to-day. 5S empowers them to change things that are not convenient for them and make them easier. 5S can easily prompt each team member in a group to report at least one improvement or safety observation per month. In a group of 20 members, you can get 240 ideas per year.

---

[9] The implementation of 5S lean tool using system dynamics approach Oleghe Omogbaia, Konstantinos Salonitisa

[10] The Application of the Toyota Production System LEAN 5S Methodology in the Operating Room Setting
Treasa 'Susie' Leming-Lee, DNP, MSN, RNa,*, Shea Polancich, PhD, RNb, Bonnie Pilon, PhD, RN-BC, NEAc

[11] https://www.researchgate.net/publication/237118519_Case_Study_on_Using_Lean_Principles_to_Improve_Turnaround_Time_and_First_Case_Starts_in_an_Operating_Room

[12] 5S methodology implementation in the laboratories of an industrial engineering university school Mariano Jiménez (a), Luis Romero (b), Manuel Domínguez (b), María del Mar Espinosa (b). a) Department of Mechanical Engineering, Technical School of Engineering – ICAI, Universidad de Comillas, Madrid, Spain. b) Design Engineering Area – Universidad Nacional de Educación a Distancia (UNED), Madrid, Spain

[13] http://www.bbc.com/travel/story/20170504-the-japanese-skill-copied-by-the-world

A Gallup study shows that lower productivity of actively disengaged workers penalizes U.S. economic performance by about $300 billion, or a figure nearly equal to the nation's defense budget.[14]

Through 5S, team members learn the importance of making a micro change every week. As a result, they become more focused because they remove obstacles that distract them, more innovative and engaged at work. Result: reduced absences, improved interactions with other teammates and improved work satisfaction.

5S is applicable in all types of companies and industries, from manufacturing plants to offices, from small to multinational businesses, from private to public sectors, all around the globe.

- Offices
- Schools
- Hospitals
- Kindergarten
- Families
(See the chapter 5S by Industry)

It's so simple, practical, and visual that well implemented, 5S can engage the operators, the managers and company owners and surprise the customers as well.

5S is a way of working, a culture that employees develop by changing their day-to-day behaviors and applying them everywhere they go.

5S at home
As a working mother, 5S always helped my family and me. Mostly, it always kept communication simple and things available to anyone. The digital age transformed not only business but also families. Poor communication, the lack of standard rules, and the poor practice of self-discipline increase the odds of fighting with your spouse and your kids for trivial things.

Disorganization and clutter contribute to increasing your stress. It's hard to know what's done or pending. Decision-making and task assignments are blurred. Who is right? It's easier to get frustrated

---

[14] https://news.gallup.com/businessjournal/439/what-your-disaffected-workers-cost.aspx

when duties are not clear. If we have the same issues at work as at home, why not use 5s at home?

You can make this a family activity so that everyone is involved in organizing where everything goes, what is needed, and what is not. Engaging everyone helps to maintain the organization through time and make it easier. Everyone will feel proud of it. Make your home mothers-in-law proof!

Now it's time to learn about the 5S more in-depth to understand how to make your environment work for you and your team.

Let's stop procrastination and start self-organization!

1S SORT

SEPARATE NEEDED FROM UNNEEDED

"Everything is found in less than 30 seconds."

In the healthcare sector, at least 44,000 Americans die each year as a result of medical errors. 40% to 50% of hospital errors take place in the operation room (OR).

Distractions and interruptions in the surgical flow are contributing factors to medical error, mostly due to unnecessary foot traffic searching for supplies, medications and medical equipment. There is usually one distraction every 10 minutes; 81% of them are unnecessary.

A neurosurgery OR implemented 5S to decrease craniotomy infection rates.

After 5S, the team reduced inventory by 68%, increased space available, reduced waste, motion, visual confusion and distractions. Infection rates decreased from 9.9 to 2.6 infections per 100 procedures, below the national benchmark.[15]

Sort is the first step in any 5S process. The term sort derives originally from the Japanese word "Seiri" which means decide what you need. When you sort, the goal is to remove unnecessary items from the room, station, or space you live or work. Then, you would be ready to carry out the other four steps.

The sorting process starts by observing your workplace or focus area from an observer point of view and trying to identify everything that you won't use in the short term. Look at all the items you have on the table or the desk (documents, tools, pens, folders), open your drawers and cabinets. Check if there are boxes or tools on the floor.

What are you going to use to work **today**? Do you have documents on your desk that you have to approve or review? Or do you have reports that you already approved last week and should be stored? Are there any tools on your desk? Why do you have them on the desk? Are you going to use them all today? Do you need to do anything with them?

Sorting is not about getting rid of everything, either. You need to be careful to ensure you will have what you need at the right time. Here I introduce the first 5S principle: **"find everything in less than 30".**

In this first step, you usually realize that there are many items that you desire to keep, but you don't need them. I am not talking about family pictures or decorations that you want to keep. Identify documents, tools or items that "you may use in the future," but realistically, you won't use it at all. The problem is that, in five years when you want to use them, you won't find them, or they will not be in good condition anymore so you will buy another anyway. Let's avoid it.

Sorting is like planning; for every minute you spend sorting, you earn an hour.

---

[15] Extracted from "The Application of the Toyota Production system Lean Lean 5S Methodology in the Operating Room Setting". Treasa "Susie" Leamng-Lee and Shea Polancich. Vanderbilt University School of Nursing https://doi.org/10.1016/j.cnur.2018.10.008

For every minute you spend sorting, you earn an hour.

If you don't sort, then you need to store it. Storing items is always expensive. You need:

- physical space that you could use for something else
- insurance for storage
- a maintenance schedule to keep the items in good shape
- transport and move it around
- regular checks to keep the inventory updated

So the more you sort, the less you store.

And these are just some of the expenses you may incur. Toyota developed the Just in Time (JIT) system to ensure you have stock only when needed. But this is not only for parts or raw material. In 5S, you think about JIT at any moment with anything.

And the highest cost of all is the cost of distracting you.

The Book "Rewire your brain"[16] explains that a more organized environment helps you focus on what needs to be done at the present moment and avoid distractions. "Chronic disorganization is a state of mental condition. We are too much associated with our environment. Keeping our things organized keeps our mind free from the thought of searching them".

Present-moment awareness boosts stress resilience and well-being and reduces accidents and mistakes. It also lowers levels of anxiety and depression. 5S is an opportunity to become more mindful of your daily tasks, reduce multitasking and focus on one task at a time.

The real challenge is how to adopt these behaviors, how to become more mindful.

As you will learn, when you get to the 5th S, you need to start small. This book will expose the 5S steps divided into 15 microsteps to make it easier and doable.

---

[16] John Hanson. *Rewire your brain*. E-book

Three main microsteps that are part of the Sorting step:
1) Develop focus and ownership
2) Sort needed from unneeded
3) Expose and remove waste

1- Develop focus and ownership

An essential part of 5S is to help team members focus and build ownership. The organization needs everybody to be involved in what's going on, engaged, and ready to report improvements everywhere, anytime. If you "own" your place, you are in the best position to decide what to keep, what to remove, and how to do it.

Delays and procrastination in decision-making are usually due to the lack of empowerment and common rules that help team members decide by themselves. Sometimes people don't feel psychologically safe to decide or are not trained to do so.

Ownership also enhances focus. A Beacon College research[17] shows that when you are asked to perform dual tasks versus being able to devote your attention to just one task reduces brain activation. Multitasking decreases concentration by as much as 20% to 40%. Similar to the OR case study, this research shows that Workplace interruptions can cause employees to take up to 27% more time to complete a task, commit up to twice as many errors, and experience up to twice the anxiety.

A starting point to promote ownership building is to assign areas to the team members, just like restaurants assign tables to waiters. Take a map or diagram, including all the departments, facilities, or rooms in the organization (also virtual folders or drives) and divide it into sections or shares that team members can "own," check image 3. You can practice this even at home: you take the kitchen, your spouse gets the bedroom, your kiddo gets the playroom.

The section includes EVERYTHING you can see: the floors, the walls, the windows, desks, tools, anything within that space. You want team members to know what they need in the area. They will be the ones to define the rules of that area as they are the most knowledgeable.

Some suggestions:
- Develop a floor plan with clear owners
- Make sure there are NO grey areas (areas nobody owns)
- Communicate the floor plan to the owners

---

[17] https://www.fastcompany.com/3060388/what-happens-in-your-brain-when-you-lose-focus

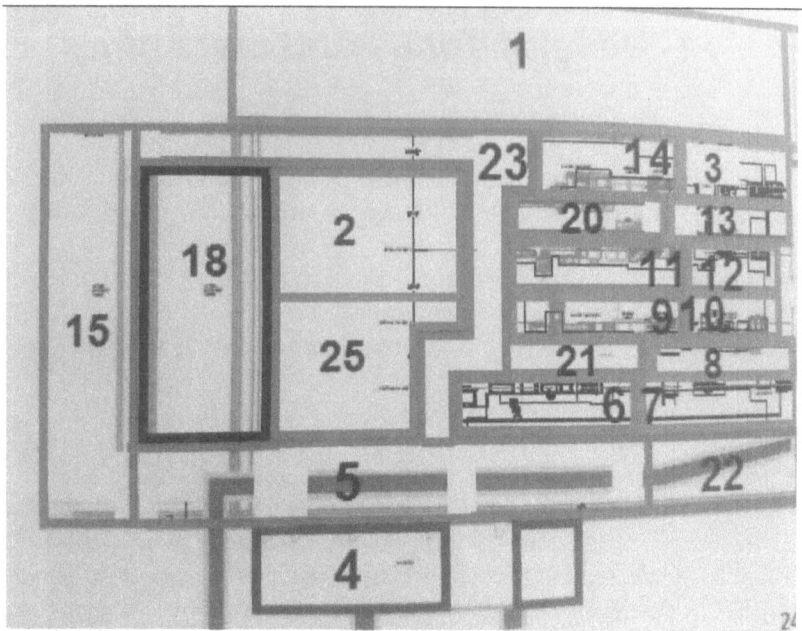

Image 3

Sometimes, associates take their space seriously without thinking about a "we" mindset (team mindset). They get rid of things they don't need by merely moving them out to someone else's area. It is not a final solution; they are just moving the problem (a.k.a procrastinating).

5S is not a zero-sum game. Everyone needs to learn to decide what to do and not just leave the decision to someone else

Toyota uses the Andon cord to communicate that there is an issue. Pleasant music sounds until you solve the problem, or it won't stop. You need a system to make sure your employees make a decision quickly and do not delay it. You can implement red lights, Andon cords, or labels to expose waste. In the end, as the owner, you will follow up to ensure waste is gone.

Deliverable microstep #1: Organization focused by area and owner.

2- Sort needed from unneeded

It's time to sort what you need to work NOW.

Let's say you have a home office. What do you need there? Which items do you usually use? How many items do you keep just in case, like documents? Do you have toys that belong to your kids or clothes? Do you have old hardware that is no longer in use? To avoid wasting precious time and money, you should quickly find the items **you need, where you need them when you need them.**

This sorting is not only physical but also virtual. If you are using your computer right now, how many sites do you have open? Aren't they consuming your computer's memory? How many are you actually consulting currently? Check them now.

Opening lots of websites at the same time or taking documents out of the drawer and leaving them out there, just in case, because "I may need it." 5S teaches us to have only what we will use now and store or close once used.

Go around your office, operating room or workstation. Wherever you work, you will call it "your area" from now on. Check all the desks, tables, boxes, shelves, open drawers and cabinets. Do you see items on the floor, under the desks, under or on top of machines? Do you have trays with various documents?

Try to set a specific temporary spot (you can even mark it with masking tape) where you will put all the items that, at first, you think you don't need.

Helpful Hints

The first walkarounds are an excellent opportunity to take pictures of the current state and compare how it used to look and how 5S changed it. Before & After images are powerful.

Now try to do a needed-not-needed check (see Image 4).

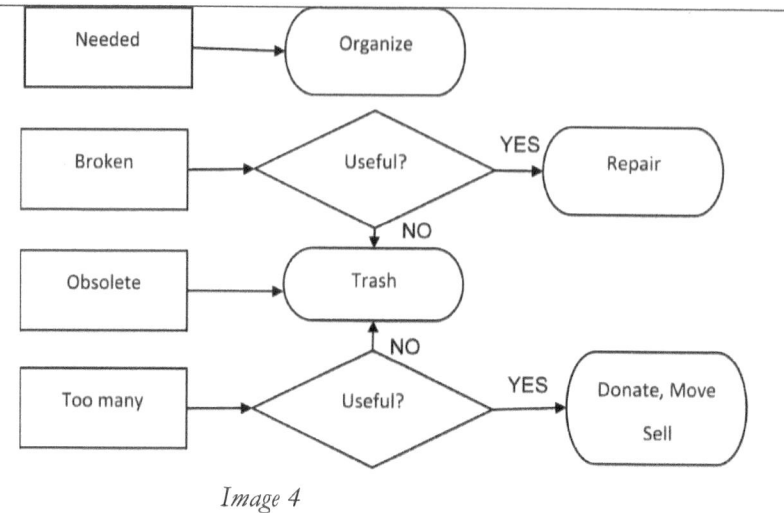

Image 4

Needed items:

Are there any items you think you may need in the future? Think again. Do you REALLY need them? Are they in the right place? Or should they be placed in another room? The go-nogo rule varies based on the product type, but you can think that if you haven't used it in the last year, you won't need it any time soon. Maybe the item is in good condition, and you don't want to throw it away. You may store it in the attic, or a shared area drawer, or even in offsite storage as you won't need it soon. You may want to give it to someone else that needs it the most.

Broken items:

Machines, tools, clothes, or equipment that are broken, damaged, or not in good condition, you need to define if they are still useful and can be repaired or not. One of the principles is to keep items "looking like brand-new". If you can get the item fixed, label it with the "DO NOT USE – TO BE REPAIRED" tag, including the date when you found it broken, to avoid other people using it. It is great to have a standard tag for this situation in places where broken items are business as usual, such as workshops or maintenance shops. In this case, some companies also have a specific area marked on the floor as "to be repaired." It is especially useful when another department from the company or a supplier can come and pick it up directly for that spot. You have the item where you need it, and everybody knows what to do with it.

Obsolete items:

You will find things that you don't need anymore. These are the ones that have a due date, like food or chemical components. It could also be a component or tool that is no longer in use. If you can spare parts that are still useful, separate them and STORE them (go to the second S). Some obsolete items may not help us but may apply to other groups within the organization, so before sorting them, make sure nobody else needs them. If they are not required, you can either throw them away, donate them, or sell them. Some companies sell metal parts or cartons to other companies. Some recycle them, sell them online, or simply donate them. Other companies prefer to store the items "just in case." If this is your case, find a place to keep them that is far away enough not to bother you in your day-to-day, it may be at the warehouse or in the last shelf of your cabinet, don't leave it visible "just in case." If possible, go back to the first step to challenge the need. If you still want to keep it, develop an inventory of these types of parts. You don't want to see them every day, but you don't forget about them either.

Too many:

Last but not least, I urge you to define what is the correct number of items that you can consider "needed." Mainly consumables, tools, instruments, or even pens in the office or silverware in the kitchen. Have you ever wondered why you have more than one blue pen on your desk? Why do you have so many tools of the same type and size in the toolbox? Here it is a good practice to estimate how many you and your team use every day and define a safety stock. Also, consider what the cost of the item itself is. What is the price of not having it at the right time? What if you run out of it? Is this an operating room where you have a life in danger? Do you have the warehouse nearby?

If you need one day to refill one item, you may want to ensure a safety stock of two days to avoid running out of it. It is just a suggestion; you need to consider where you get it, the risk, the cost and the variability for getting the item on time. You can use visual management to help you order more parts at the right time (4S – Standardize).

Simply avoid having 100 pens within reach when you only use one per month. You can have just two and store the other 98 somewhere else. It is the same for a purse or a toolbox. You can always refill when you finish the shift, add it as a routine (4S – Standardize). Remember that you may want that extra space for other really needed items for every single space count.

Image 5

The inventory

As a reminder of all the items you need, design an inventory sheet. An inventory is like a shopping list (virtually on your phone or physically on a sheet of paper) so that you never run out of what matters (hence you can find it in less than 30 seconds). You know how many you have and how many you need to buy with this list. You can also use visual tools to remind everyone what you need to keep, like tool shapes or shades, foam or plastic dividers, hangers or transparent bins (4S – Standardize).

The most effective way to plan how to get rid of waste and how to work on improvements and suggested actions is to use a report. The action plan is a feature to report all the things you need to remove, trash, move, buy or repair (action items). Whatever you plan to do to 5S your section, write it down in your action plan. It will help you organize your pending tasks so that you are ready to roll when you have a spare minute.

Action plans

The action plan is a set of action items that the team members identify to resolve in their sub-sections. It is a to-do list. It could be a hand-written list, an excel spreadsheet or an online list using an action plan template. See image 6 as an example of an action plan. Ideally, include: date, name of the section or department, finding, what needs to be done, who has to do it, the estimated date for doing it, progress (25%, 50%, 75% or 100%), closing date and add extra space for additional info.

You can go to www.Theweculture.com to download our App and find a sample of an action plan.

You can also have as an action plan a simple three-column list: To-do, Doing, and Done.

#	DATE	SECTION	FINDING	WHAT NEEDS TO BE DONE	WHO	ESTIMATED CLOSING	PROGRESS %	CLOSING DATE	EXTRA INFO
1									
2									
3									
4									
5									
6									
7									

Image 6

Action items

Action items are the individual tasks listed in your action plan. When you start practicing the micro-steps and following the three 5S principles, you will constantly see things that can be improved. For example, you can't find a tool, it has a home, but you can't find it there. The principle "find everything in less than 30 seconds" is not followed. So your action item will be something like, x tool can't be found in less than 30". The proposed solution could be getting a better place to store the device or discussing why it was not returned to its home in a team meeting.

This discussion helps to let everybody in your team know that it is important to respect the agreed storing locations and ensure what we use is ready for someone else to use after ourselves.

An action item typically includes the date it was found, the description of the finding, a recommendation of what needs to be done to consider the item closed, who will solve the problem (or at least who is the owner of the issue), the planned date and the actual date to close it. Example of action items:

- X tool is not working properly
- The floor under the machine x is dirty
- X tool has no identified home
- There is no cleaning schedule at sub-section x
- There is no maintenance schedule for machine x
- There is a leak under machine X
- There are various documents on the desk, not organized or prioritized

The 5S committee (SEE the chapter HOW TO SUPPORT THE IMPLEMENTATION - Roles) can define the standards of the action items. For instance, when you find an issue that will be solved right away, do you solve it and include it as an action item or just solve it and not include it? An action plan is an excellent tool to help prioritize action items and a tracking tool to measure improvements. If the action plan is used as a monitoring tool, it is helpful to include all the improvements, no matter how small or fast you have solved them. For individuals, it is a way to help self-organize, engage and avoid procrastination.

Deliverable microstep #2: Inventory of needed and unneeded items.

3- Expose and remove waste

Now that you sorted out what you don't need, eliminate, move, donate, sell, or trash it. Never leave anything unattended in your area. Benjamin Franklin once said, "Never leave till tomorrow that which you can do today." Leaving the space free of waste is part of finishing your job. If you don't do it today, you forget it later, or someone makes a different decision for you. Leaving the task for someone else is not self-organization; it is called procrastination. Even if you know it's broken, other people accessing your area may try to use it. Never assume someone else will do it. If in doubt, move it out or label it.

To help your mind focus on what is essential and requires your attention, you need to remove the rest of the items you don't need from your sight. What you don't need but still is in your way every day only keeps your brain busy. See how much waste you can accumulate in image 7.

Image 7

Identify your items using the guide on image 8.

You probably have a desk, a workbench, or a tool board where you should find only the items that you need to use in the next hour or two. (A) For the rest of the items that you may need this week, you can have them in drawers or cabinets within your reach (B). The ones that you use monthly or maybe next year (C or D), you can have them in shared area cabinets, warehouses, storerooms, or even in off-site storage.

If it has been around for more than one year without being used, likely, you will not need it any time soon, so move it out (F).

In the previous step, you sorted many broken or obsolete items easily, but probably you still have many other items that you considered as "needed" and could be removed too. Some people say, "well, I haven't used this document for two years, but I may need it one day," so they put it in the needed category but still never use it again. Try to think if this could be you, and how you could sort more efficiently. Based on the amount of space you have for storage, I strongly recommend you consider the frequency of use to make decisions and define rules for the entire team.

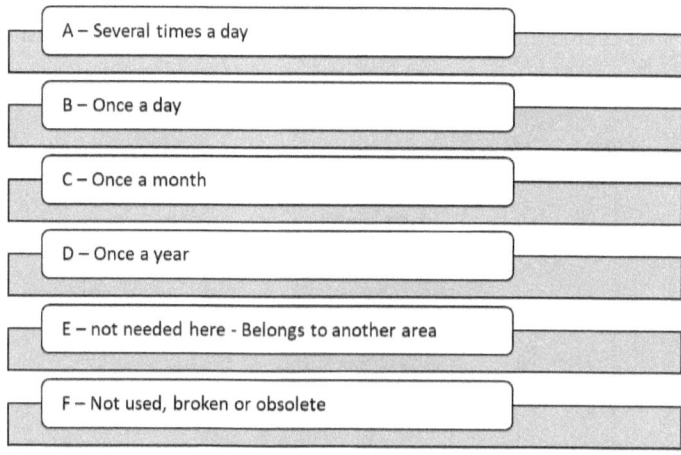

Image 8

Slow-moving inventory

Every document your team creates should have a removal date since the creation date. For example, invoices may be useful for ten years for legal purposes (every company and industry varies, so please check your legal department here), so you may want to store them based on the removal date, ten years from now.

The same happens with digital documents (check your desktop and look for documents or direct access links posted right there). If you organize them based on this date, then it is much easier to get rid of them at the right time. You need to know the removal date of all the documents you create.

Labs, for instance, have tests, samples, consumables and preparations that are good for a certain period and no longer needed after that date. Make sure they are stored so you can easily identify the ones to throw away. Depending on your process, you can use colors, numbers, or storage locations for the different years, months, or days of creation.

Theme parks have wristbands that they give to registered customers, and they use different colors every day to make sure people have paid.

Laboratory Case Study

The lab was about to be redesigned and rebuilt. The storage room was too small for all the samples they needed to store. Many bottles and containers were stacked on the shelves, going way over the weight limits. Some looked like they were about to fall off the shelf, definitely a potential safety incident. They couldn't take any risks; the samples had to be kept safe for legal purposes.

When implementing 5S, on the first step of sorting, they realized many bottles were already due and could be removed from the lab storage room. The system to empty old containers was not accurate enough; apparently, some had been missed. They decided to eliminate all the bottles older than a year. They labeled all the shelves showing the month and lot number to make it easy to locate when needed or to identify when they had to be taken out. A process was put in place to empty the old containers once a month. They also red-defined the weight limit signs. Instead of showing the weight in absolute numbers, they showed in "number of bottles or cans" so that it was easier to detect when the shelf was overweight. The storage room also contained ladders, old machines and other items that were not needed in there. All these items that did not belong to the lab were removed. Extra shelves were installed in the saved space.

The lab now contained only the legally required containers, no more, no less. The samples were found faster when required and removed faster after a year. The storage room was not replaced; now, it was big enough.

Slow-moving inventory takes up valuable shelf space and can drain your facility's efficiency. You don't want stock hanging around too long. It takes up space and workforce to maintain it, apart from the risk you are taking for something that doesn't have value (insurance is needed anyway). Remember that whatever you have, you need to keep it in good condition as per the third S Shine that you will get to know soon.

The red tag process

Usually, you find out things you don't need or can't use anymore, but they are expensive, or they are activated/registered in the company ERP. It is usually the case of parts, machines, documents, or inventory. You can't just eliminate them; you will need to remove them from the ERP system, too, even if they are just donated to an employee or thrown away. Here is where you probably need management clearance first.

You have to define a standardized process (4S – Standardize) to deal with this type of item so that employees immediately know what to do with them when they find them.

Depending on the type of product, it may be challenging to decide. Sometimes it's a one-time event, or the item is costly and may impact the balance sheet.

The recommendation is to use RED TAGS (image 9) to flag them. Red tags may have different formats. You need to define and show why the item has a red label (obsolete, broken, not required etc.), the date, the owner or who made that decision, and what needs to be done (waiting for management decision, for example). Some companies have a particular area for red tag items so that managers know where to go for approval.

The process can allow other departments access to this "red tag area" to borrow some of those items. Red tag items can also remain in the original locations, keeping the tag and listed into a master file shared with other departments.

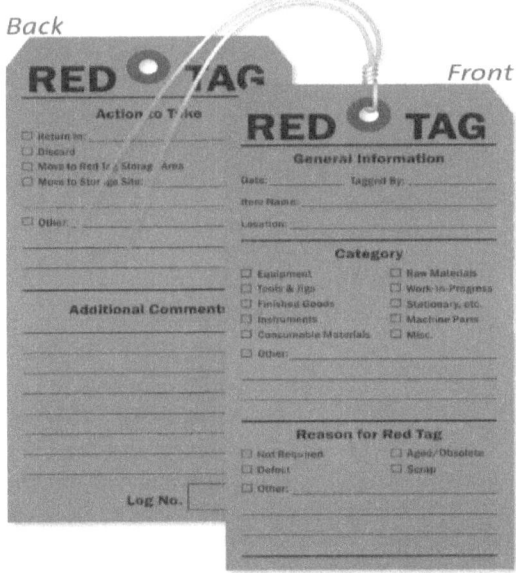

Image 9

Getting rid of assets is usually very time-consuming, so a well-defined red tag process (4S – Standardize) should help members of the organization speed things up.

It is also good to assign a red tag owner company-wide if the company has several red-tagged items, especially at the beginning of the 5S implementation. The responsible will help to push management approvals or streamline the process as needed. For example, if you do periodic 5S Committee meetings (5S CONCEPTS – Team routines), the red tag owner can report pending red tag items during this meeting to ensure visibility of the waste.

Deliverable microstep #3: Waste removed or Red Tagged.

Implementation Step 1: SORT

✓ Choose a section to start and organize a walkaround
✓ Take pictures of the current state
✓ Prepare an inventory
✓ Prepare an action plan
✓ Divide areas by owners
✓ Remove unneeded items
✓ Red tag unnecessary items that require approval

Audit Guide 1S

1) There is no trash on the floor, under equipment or furniture
2) Waste organized by type (metal, paper, plastic, oil etc.)
3) Unneeded articles identified and included in a follow-up system like a red tag.
4) Action items reported in an action plan.
5) Items identified based on the frequency of use.
6) There are no items needed in the sector located in other areas
7) There are before & after pictures
8) There is an inventory of needed and unneeded items
9) It is easy to identify an unneeded item from one needed
10) The workplace divided into sections with owners

How to practice sorting in your day-to-day?

The place or things I use the most are the first that I 5S (yes, I will use "5S" as a verb). My bedroom and my home office. It helped me focus on what matters to me. Assign owners to areas and shelves to your family members.

If you live in a small apartment, you will appreciate this step. Go room by room, and separate what is needed every day from what is unneeded. Open every drawer, tackle every cabinet, and sort them. If there is something you don't need or have not been using in the last year: trash it out, move it to another location (a basement, for example, or a place where you can use it more often), donate it or sell it.

You may be storing food that is no longer in good condition. Or maybe you are storing food in the main compartment that you will not use now, but in the next six months (such as fondant for birthday cakes) while you need the space for something else you use more often. Take the time to organize your pantry, fridge and freezer. Define what is required in the short term, and store somewhere else what is not.

If you have kids, they probably have toys stored everywhere. Throw away, donate, or save the ones the kids don't use anymore and define specific locations for the ones they use. You can have a storage location in their room, and another one in the kitchen, as long as they are in charge of using and putting away.

Sorting takes time, especially if you get attached to things. You always think, "I may need it later." So, procure to trash things right away when you find them unfit for use.

To avoid thinking twice, I always keep a trash can nearby. You find it, you trash it, done. For example, I have a small trash can over the counter in the kitchen, so whenever I break an egg or cut an onion, I immediately trash the leftovers without even moving. I also have a trashcan next to the table, so I just get rid of the leftovers without even getting to the sink when I finish eating. Sorting what I don't need immediately saves a lot of my time to sort later.

5S your mind

Use the sort principles to remove from your mind harmful thoughts that simply waste your time. Meditation and mindfulness help you reduce recurring thoughts about the future or the past that blur your mind. It helps remain in the present moment.

When you are distracted with worries, you tend to leave issues unresolved, forget where you store your items and are more prone to accidents and mistakes. For example, if you leave an empty box on the shelf, someone else will have to trash it. If you leave a broken tool unattended, someone may get hurt using it. Being aware of how you work and how it impacts others helps you work in a more careful way, more respectful to others, and enables you to improve your self-organization.

Every time you use an item, decide right away what to do with it. Think about receipts, post-its, clothes, tools, anything. Have you already used it and you don't need it anymore? Eliminate it right away. Do you need to keep it? Sort it right away, and then go to the next Step: Store.

*Download the We Culture app for
more free resources and training courses*

www.theweculture.com

2S STORE

ARRANGE FOR EASE OF USE

"A home for everything and everything in its home"

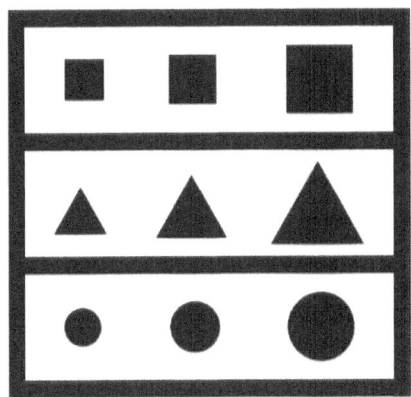

The club had a workshop where everything was repaired. Of course, club members didn't have access to this workshop. Nevertheless, the organization's executive committee had defined that if they could apply 5S to the workshop, they would provide a better service to the members. You entered that room and almost immediately could start working there. All the tools were identified. All the shelves had been modified to have the specific height required for the items they were holding. Paint cans and brushes were used less frequently, so they were stored under the stairs, which was difficult to access but perfect for items not often needed. There was even a particular area on the floor for items "to be repaired." Any department could bring to the workshop items to repair and simply store them in that area so that the workers could fix them. Close to the door, there was a shelf for repaired items to be retrieved. No further communication was needed. Things got done seamlessly.

The second step of 5S is "store" (or set in order), which derives from the Japanese term *Seiton*. It means organization.

Here comes the second 5S principle: **"A home for everything and everything in its home."** This phase focuses on placing the items deemed essential back into the workstation or area in a specific, well-organized manner. The objective is to find the most efficient homes for the tools and objects within a space to do your job better. All necessary items must have a home to be found and ready when needed.

Every time team members have to search for a tool to complete their jobs, time is wasted, and the business loses money.

Imagine the importance of well-organized tools in emergency rooms. Doctors need to have their most frequently needed tools and equipment on hand and easily accessible to help save their patients' lives. Logical organization paired with knowledge of where tools and supplies are could make the difference between life and death.

Organize all tools, equipment, files, data, material, and resources for quick, accessible location and use. Identify everything based on:

- Safety: they will not fall or hurt anyone
- Quality: they will not mix up
- Efficiency: time will not be lost searching for things

The three microsteps to implement store are:
4) Prioritize what you need
5) Define a home for ease of use
6) Store back immediately after use

4- Prioritize what you need

You need to be able to retrieve things quickly when you need them. It's time to determine where and when you need the items to allow for an efficient workflow.

Check every item you often use if it is in the right place. Ask your team:

- Who will use it?
- How often?
- When do you use it?

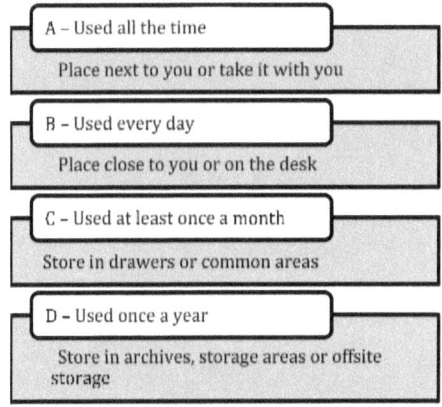

Image 10

As you can see in image 10, what you use all the time (A), you store it as close to you as possible. If you are a doctor, you place your stethoscope around your neck and your pens in your pockets. If you are a mechanic, you get a tool belt.

What you use every day (B), but maybe just once a day, you can store in your desktop drawers, a purse, or a toolbox that you take with you everywhere you go. When you have various drawers and shelves, you have to identify the priority for each of them. Which shelves are the easiest for you to reach? The top ones? The bottom ones? That desktop build-in ones?

What you use at least once a month (C), you don't need to take with you every day. Good examples are invoices that you need to pay once a month or tools for monthly activities. You can keep them in an office cabinet or a top shelf.

You may use some items pretty often, but you don't need to keep all the stock in the same place. You can have a pile close to you for everyday use and restock once a month.

For example, let's say you print documents every day. You can save a stack of paper close to the printer and the printer close to where you work while keeping a more extensive stock of paper in a closet. You can do a refill every month, set to buy automatically every month to avoid maintaining inventory, or you can define a safety stock "mark" that will remind you when to restock. Learn more about this in the 4S chapter, STANDARDIZE.

Deliverables microstep #4: Items prioritized by frequency.

5- Define a home for ease of use

This microstep is the habit of always organizing objects in a functional way, which allows you to immediately find what is needed when it is needed and especially how it is needed.

Now that you have defined what you need within reach, decide what best place to store it is, choose "a home."

What is "home"? The home is the location where you are going to store the item while you are not using it. Once you use it, you put it back in the same place.

For the sake of 5S, we show respect to anybody and anything. Everyone is important, and everything is important too. So the same way as you always (at least ideally) return home once you finish your job, every object has to get back home once its job is done.

That is the only way to find it the next time you need it. The home is a known location for everyone else. It is not a home just because you say so, "I have always stored it here, so this the home." It is "the home" once you identified it or made it clear to everyone else what it is. Ask your team members, and ask yourself:

- Is this object placed in the right place regarding its weight?
- Is this object placed in the right place regarding its size?
- Is this object placed in the right place to maintain the quality of its specifications?
- Is this object placed in the right place to ensure the location is safe?

What to take into consideration

In the previous step, you considered the frequency of use. Now think about the space available, the weight, the distance from where it will be used.

Once you identify what you need, you also plan how many you need. You did this in the previous step (1S – Sort). Now measure or at least estimate the available space and the necessary space for the product to ensure productivity, quality and safety.

Project how much space you will need in the future if the production varies, and what is the likelihood of this happening. For example, is it an object easy to move in case plans change?

Frequency

The objects that you use more frequently should be stored in easy-to-access locations, as discussed in microstep #4 "Prioritize what you need."

Weight

Heavy objects have to be in a location that makes it easier to handle them. If you store them on the top shelves, there might be more risk of falling from the top than being located at the floor level. Light objects can also be hard to handle, such as polyethylene, cotton, or certain paper types. You may need to accommodate in a location that prevents them from spreading and falling, probably within arms reach so that you can see what is inside.

Quantity

If the item is only one of a kind, it may be easier to find a location. What happens when there are many of the same kind? It's usually better to accommodate the same items in the same location, but sometimes for your convenience, you may spread and locate where you need them the most. You may use a mop and disinfecting wipes to clean at home. You can keep the mop, which is big and probably humid, in one specific place, maybe next to the washing machine. Then, you can have various packages of disinfecting wipes next to where you need them the most: at the bathroom and in the kitchen. The packages are usually small and dry, so there is no danger of contamination.

Do not have them in various locations only because of poor planning. It will make it difficult for you to analyze when you need to buy more if you have different locations for them, and you don't even know where they are. If you choose to have various locations, you can identify them with numbers to remember to refill them all.

Distance

The home needs to be close to where the item will be used. That's why you usually keep your toothbrush, soap and shampoo in the bathroom, right? Yes, it makes sense, though this is not always the case.

Sometimes process change and prioritization of use changes too. You may have bought a board to track your goals, so now you use a board marker every day. You used to store the marker in a drawer. Now that you are using it more often, you can attach it to a magnet to keep it next to the board.

It would help if you adapted the home immediately after changing a process to reduce your effort. Moving around is expensive. Not only for the time it takes but also for the dangers it entails. You may fall in the way or get distracted. In addition, you may need to stretch your body. For example, in a kitchen, you may have cupboards with various shelves. You should make sure you put regular-use cups, glasses, and plates on the shelves within arms reach and store "party" plates of silverware in a different location; it doesn't have to be easy to reach because you don't use them often.

Distance may not seem to be an apparent significant issue. Team members usually say, "it takes me just one minute to get back." Well, if you estimate one minute per twenty times a day per 5 coworkers, you spend one hundred minutes in total. If you get a satellite location right next to each team member, it only takes ten seconds to grab the object. Then you only spend one minute once a day refilling the container. How much time would you be saving? Ten by twenty by five coworkers, it takes less than 17 minutes of work plus five more minutes for each employee to refill. It takes twenty-two minutes in total compared to one hundred.

Some companies have someone responsible for restocking storage locations. Other companies don't even have an owner for the warehouse; it is all self-service.

It is your call to decide what method better serves your purpose, but it is valuable to review your process and see it with a different lens. I can tell you that If only one person is restocking or approving it, you have a bottleneck when there is a lot of work or this person is absent. Team member autonomy usually helps to prevent bottlenecks. Ask your coworkers. They may have other ideas. They may all be working in different ways, discuss which one is more efficient.

Image 11

Quality

You need to make sure that the home will ensure no mix-up with other items or no damage to the quality of the product.

Some items need to be stored at a specific temperature like food or pharmaceutical; some others simply need a bit of shade. Sometimes you need to use foam around the object to keep it from breaking. Using the safety data sheet (SDS) to handle and store chemical information is always useful.

Depending on the product, the details of how you store are critical. For example, make expensive parts or tools like a caliper secure by keeping them in properly controlled areas with limited access, with a lock or a closed container.

You may have more affordable items like wrenches or screwdrivers that you may want to expose for ease of access.

Damaged items and non-conforming products should also be segregated in specific locations to avoid mixing them with the working products. Like in image 12 below, you can define a home for the items "to be repaired."

Image 12

Many companies are concerned with leaving objects exposed instead of locked down because items get lost. However, allowing items to be exposed is a mindset change as part of 5S. Once employees learn to put things down after using them, exposing items as much as possible is the obvious solution to ensure they don't get lost.

Safety
Consider applying ergonomic techniques to promote safety and efficiency. The location you choose has to be appropriate for the type of object. Aisles, workplaces, and hazardous areas should be marked as part of this microstep to prevent accidents while team members work. Working areas can be marked with floor lines or signs, indicating status "work in progress," "stop" or "being repaired." As you will see in microstep #11 Make the rules visible, visual management is critical to enforce proper storage and safety.

You may need to store flammable aerosols in a fire-resistant storage cabinet or inside a storage room rated for fire resistance as per OSHA rules. Different objects have different safety considerations that need to be reviewed to find the best place. Team members should be trained and encouraged to check the safety data sheet (SDS) for handling and storage information. If parts and materials are hazardous, label them clearly so that everyone knows of the danger.

Sometimes the item is not hazardous per se, but the way you store it makes it dangerous. A heavy tool should not be placed on a high shelf. Again, consider the weight and size to prevent items from falling. It is also best to mark or have a sign showing height, weight, and quantity limits when working on shelves or pallets. Cables are not hazardous if they are well maintained. They may become a threat when the ones damaged are not organized properly. Cables should not be visible or cause a trip hazard or electrocution hazard.

Efficiency

For efficiency and productivity, how you store and identify items can help you. Use labels, bins and trays to indicate what is "pending to be done," "in progress," "due soon," or "for approval." Keep the rest of the documentation in drawers or cabinets so that you can only see what you need to do. These indicators also help you redistribute work as required to improve the workflow quickly when working in teams.

If "pending" bins or trays are more filled than others, that may indicate either someone is too slow or too much work. You can reassign the workflow. During shift changes, it helps to communicate what needs to be done, approved, or re-worked. When someone is suddenly absent, anyone should be able to take over the desk, knowing what's pending.

The kanban method takes advantage of this visual organization of tasks. During a period of time, let's say a week, team members can choose what task to accomplish from a team list of tasks pre-selected. You can only keep one item in the DOING bucket. Then, once the job is accomplished, you need to move immediately to the DONE. You can learn more about Kanban in the chapter TOOLS TO COMPLEMENT 5S.

How to identify the locations

To identify the identification and location of objects, use labels, colors, signs, diagrams, containers, and before and after pictures to facilitate finding everything and keeping it as is.

Tools and devices must be labeled or outlined in the most effective position to help you use them. Trash cans, restrooms, extinguishers, and cleaning supply areas can have wall signs indicating where they are so that they can be easily located. Some companies buy tool boards for every workstation, which in some cases could be helpful, but not in others. Sometimes you only have a couple of tools at a specific location.

Image 13

Shadow labeling, floor labeling, tagging, and outlining communicate the exact spot where equipment belongs. It also identifies how it should be stored, as you will see in the next microstep. You can also identify where people should be using different clothes or accessories. For example, in a food manufacturing plant, there are some areas where you may have to use gloves or face masks. You may paint the walls or floors to identify the area, or simply have a sign identifying the location and the required PPE's (personal protective equipment).

Identification has to be clear for everyone. Kindergarteners, for instance, use their pictures to know where to store their backpacks and coats. Airplanes use standard universal characters signs and videos instead of words in many cases to ensure there are no language barriers.

Signaling the location of everything that can be moved helps quickly detect any abnormality. Trash cans, boxes, chairs and tables are commonly shadowed, labeled on the floor to identify their location.

You can use shelves, boxes, and containers to help you use all the space available. Usually, shelves are not the exact height we need, and you tend to leave a lot of space not utilized.

Move the shelves as needed to adjust precisely to the size of the items stored.

Sometimes it is useful to remove the objects from the original box. Use transparent containers instead to see the amount and type of content. You can mark the container with a red line as an indicator to refill. If the shelves are high or the items are small, stackable containers or drawers help duplicate or triplicate the space using full height. Drawers help to use full depth.

Image 14 Before

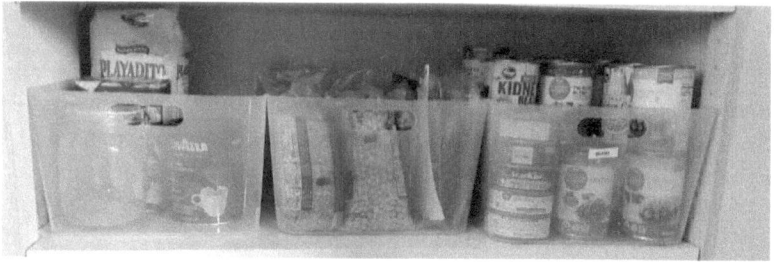

Image 15 After

Drawers and organizers are handy to help use as much space as possible while keeping the objects visible. Remember to ask the owners to open drawers and cabinets when auditing sectors. Drawers commonly accommodate food, documentation no longer needed, and tons of pens (yes, do not laugh here, check your drawers first!). They also hide precious objects like money, keys, and other everyday use stuff like calculators or post-its. All these items should be organized in a way that, when you open the drawer, you (and everyone else) know exactly where to find them. First, sort (1S – Sort) to remove unneeded. Then use small containers and dividers. Here the rule is, organize the drawer in such a way that anybody can open it anytime, even when you are away, and you will not feel ashamed of what they see.

Organizing it "my way" is not enough; you need to organize things in a way that is easy for everyone else to find. Spaces at home or work are shared unless you live on your own; they are not just yours. Let's remember it every time you leave your workstation to respect each other.

Helpful Hints

Hint #1: storing doesn't need to be expensive. You can buy containers, dividers, drawers and boards. But don't make it your priority. First, you realize how much more space you have available when you sort. Then, to classify the area, you can recycle empty containers, build boxes or dividers, add transparent sheets, use tape to mark refilling points. You can even build your own canvas.

Hint #2: before painting, use masking tape to test if this is the right place, like an MVP (minimum viable product). Sometimes you think it is, but in the day-to-day use doesn't seem comfortable. Let the "customer" test the location for a week or so. Once the test has been approved, use paint to mark it. Check if there are any company standards in terms of colors and formats.

Deliverables microstep #5: Homes identified.

6- Store back immediately after use

This microstep is the last habit you need to learn of the step Store. This habit reminds you to get things done: store everything in its place right after you use it, or the job is not finished.

The 'Store' step has to do with finding the object and how ready you find it. If the item has a home, you know where it is, but someone took it, broke it, or misplaced it, it is not ready for you to use. Finding it in the proper condition, ready to use, is what we strive to achieve. If you need batteries to use it, you need to have the batteries ready to use (charged) in the same place. If you need a charger, you need to have the charger in the same location or close, or you need to have directions on how to use the charger, where it is located, and how to keep the item charged after you use it. (4S – Standardize).

Buckets and cleaning supplies (3S – Shine) also need to have a home. Every time you use them, you need to put them back to where they belong. But the trick is that you have to leave them empty and ready to use.

Let's say you used a bucket to clean an oily floor. Once you finish, you need to store it in the same place, clean. If it is full of water or oily, it is not ready to use. The job is not done until all the items used are clean, charged, inspected or maintained, and stored in their respective homes.

Storing the items in the proper position also helps to ensure ease of use.

When you finish dinner, you can put the dishes in the sink or put them directly into the dishwasher machine.

When you go to bed and leave your slippers at the bedside, just leave them in such a way that you can quickly put them on when you wake up. If you take the slippers off when standing up, you probably leave them in the opposite position. But if you change your habit to take them off when you sit down at the bed, you will leave them ready to use. Do you see it? No extra steps; you just adjust the process to reduce extra work and ensure use readiness.

It may sound "too picky." The trick is that, at home, you may not be saving any money, but the fact of "exercising" your self-organization habits makes you better at work too. Imagine how much your company could save if all the team members would think about all these details in every task they perform.

It is not just about time but also about safety. For example, when you store a knife, considering the orientation of the blade is a matter of safety.

When the orientation of an object is critical, the storage location is critical too. Boxes, drums, totes, and any other container should be placed so that you can see the label correctly. Image 16 shows how you can define the standard for the labels. You also have to put the objects ergonomically, that is, in a way adapted to the way you work. You can use a picture (see 4S – Standardize) to show the way the box should be stored. Or, you can use *poka-yoke* or error-proof techniques (see TOOLS TO COMPLEMENT 5S) to make it difficult to store the wrong way. Foam, shades, and individual containers help to ensure storage is safe and sound.

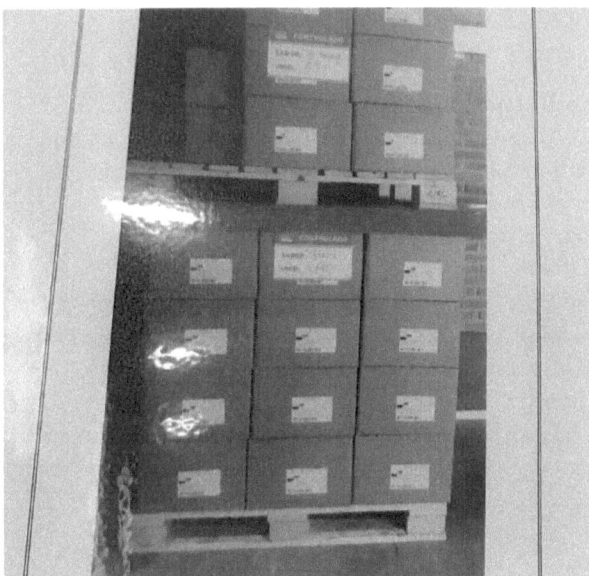

Image 16

Helpful hints

Hint #1: You shouldn't wait for the end of the day, or worse, the end of the week, to put everything back to its home. The magic of the Store phase is that you learn to store as you go. Use and store, use, and store. Daycares teach this to babies since they are very young. They use one toy, they store it. Teachers remind kids to store everything in its place before starting the next game. Organizing everything at the end of the day should not be a headache; most items should have already been restored to their original location when used.

Deliverable microstep #6: Everything stored away before finishing the job.

Implementation Step 2: STORE

✓ Organize things based on the frequency of use

✓ Define a home for everything considering the space needed based on future usage, frequency of use by you and others in your site, distance to the place of use and weight, and safety hazards.

✓ Get the job done by storing everything in its place immediately after use

Audit Guide 2S

1. Items are located based on their frequency of use, weight, size, etc.
2. Distance and movements considered to store items
3. Every item has a specific location to be stored
4. Every item in its place
5. Items put away immediately after use
6. Damaged items or non-conforming product segregated
7. Aisles, workplaces, tools and equipment locations are marked
8. Articles organized by color, letter, number or any other type of classification
9. Height, quantity limits and object orientation clearly marked
10. Cables not visible or able to cause a tripping or electrocution hazard

How to practice storing in your day-to-day?

Now that you have sorted out what was not needed, and you decided what you needed, store it. Everything should have a home. Label that home, or make it obvious for everyone to find it right there. Obvious means even for your kids. Use pictures or drawings if you need them.

Labeling is an extraordinary communication tool for visitors. Labels help them to help you keep your house organized and things in place. When they find utensils easily, they feel more comfortable, like at home, and the stress is reduced. When my mom comes to visit, she keeps asking for certain items or keeps putting them in different places unless I label them. Once I identify what she cares more about, I make sure it's easily visible and available for her to avoid any friction.

You can use transparent drawers for a playroom to make it easier for everyone, even neighbors that come to play, to find out how to organize things back. Do the 30 seconds test: If you need more than 30 seconds to find something, it is not in the right place; find it a home. Ensure the home is convenient for everybody using it, is safe (heavyweights should not be placed on top shelves), and keeps the product quality (like kitchen stuff that cannot get wet or have specific due dates).

- Store the items that have short due dates and need to be consumed earlier closer to the door, or label them with clear due dates or red tags.

- You may need to rearrange items. Sometimes you realize you have items in the fridge that could be stored somewhere else and still be safe. Prioritize your items so that they are in the best possible location, considering the frequency of use, who needs to use them or access them and who doesn't and where it is the safer location to keep quality intact.

- Organize items by category, and label them if necessary. That way, you know where all the cans are, where all the flours are, where all the dairy items are, etc. It helps you cook more efficiently and define when to re-stock.

- To get more space out of the same cabinet, just be mindful of how you organize your items. Usually, there is a lot of space on the back of the shelf, or its height is not fully used. You can use square containers (transparent ones are desired) to pile up more items and use the full height of the shelve. Measure it before buying the containers to be more efficient. You can also move the shelves to adjust the size as needed.

- Use Kanban or checklists to keep up with the inventory and avoid frequent check-ins to the supermarket.

- Prioritize everything you need based on the frequency of use and decide the most convenient location. Have everything handy before you start working. Keep it simple and visible so that everyone in the organization helps you keep it organized.

Image 17 – Before

Image 18 - After

5S your mind

Prioritize the thoughts you need to succeed. YOU already got rid of the limiting beliefs by sorting. Now you can organize your growth ideas by writing them down. Keep a journal, a to-do list, a board or an action plan that helps you "store" your thoughts time-wise: to be done today, next week or later. It will help you reduce your anxiety and stress about "having a lot to do." Keep this to-do list close to you always. I use the phone during the day and a notepad next to my bed during the night.

Last but not least, discipline yourself to always store away after use, tools and thoughts! That is, once you put into practice your idea, mark it done! That's how you get a feeling of accomplishment and satisfaction.

Once you organize your things and thoughts, all you have to do is make sure you expose problems that may make you procrastinate. How? Go to the next Step: Shine.

Download the We Culture app for more free resources and training courses

www.theweculture.com

3S SHINE

SET A NEW LEVEL OF CLEANLINESS TO SPOT HIDDEN
PROBLEMS

"Keep everything like brand-new"

There was an oil leak on line 4. Operators said it had been there for more than five years. They said they had reported it to maintenance several times, but they couldn't repair it. It was too expensive. The oil was everywhere, so pig mats were replaced frequently to contain it. I could tell employees were frustrated, as this leak was a source of many issues, including unsafe behaviors. A picture was taken and shown in several training sessions and committee meetings with managers. The problem was finally solved during the first year of the 5S implementation.

The third step of 5S is shine. This phase focuses on shining and cleaning everything to spot hidden problems (oil leaks, water drops, etc.).This step honors the 3rd 5S principle, **"The workplace and its items look brand-new."**

Cleaning is part of everyone's job, not just by janitors. Employees clean the areas and machinery that they regularly use. Additionally, they also clean common areas as if they would have visitors around soon. No job is complete unless the items used for the job are put away properly.

For instance, the Japanese remove their shoes before entering their homes to prevent contamination from the outside. Even ambulance personnel take their shoes before seeing an urgent care patient.

Cleaning is not just a matter of image; it is a matter of good communication. Then, you can detect errors easily!

Looking *brand-new*

Shine is all about making the workplace, and the items inside look *brand-new*. It doesn't mean that you need to buy all new items to implement 5S the right way. On the contrary, it means that you want to clean and repair all the issues to get back to how they looked when you just bought them. Set this state as the starting point or standard to take care of them in every use.

There used to be a carpet on the floor in a company I visited. It had never been removed before to clean the floor, even though it was small. When it was removed for the first time when we were doing 5S, there was a mark on the floor around it that couldn't be removed with basic cleaning products. Through time, the floor had gotten damaged. Neither the surface nor the carpet looked brand-new. What would it take to make them shine again? Should you replace them? Should you clean them?

Image 19

Some other items may be more expensive to replace, like a lab grinder/polisher. Should you send them to a supplier to repair them? Should you paint it?

How you plan the shine phase depends on:

- How critical is the item: is the product quality affected by this item?
- How expensive is the item: can you still use it as is? It may not meet the 5S standards, but the team agrees this is not a good time to invest in improving it.
- How the item is working: even if it doesn't look brand-new, is it still working properly?
- How much do you want to spend: you can spend time repairing and cleaning it, or pay to fix it? Is it something that can be done within the budget? Can the employees do it? Do you need specific expertise? How much time do you need? How much time can the item be down? Can you replace it in the meantime?

Hence, there are many ways to decide how to accomplish shine. It is mainly up to the team to determine what is desired vs. what is required.

Every tiny little area that is not shining can be the root cause of a more significant issue in the future. Would you like to go to a restaurant where the cook or the waiters look dirty? Would you like to see a doctor stained with blood? It is part of the job to work so that things don't get dirty.

Do not get dirty in the first place!

The three microsteps to implement shine are:

7) Assign responsibilities for maintenance
8) Expose complex issues
9) Find the root cause

7- Assign responsibilities for maintenance

There is no better way to keep something clean than to prevent it from getting dirty in the first place. How do you prevent it? By assigning clear owners for the maintenance of each location/item.

Of course, everyone in your team will be complaining, seriously wondering why they need to clean, as it is not part of their job description. What about the cleaning staff? What about maintenance? Their complaint may look accurate and fair, though it is also fair to realize that you are the most knowledgeable about what your section needs. Users know what is going on in their areas. They know what is dirty and probably understand why it is dirty. Even though cleaning responsibilities may be assigned to a team dedicated only to cleaning and maintaining, it is vital to involve the operations personnel. They all need to sit together to decide what is required, how frequently, what standard is required, what is considered acceptable, and what is the best time to clean or do maintenance work.

At home, we distributed the responsibilities of maintenance. My husband "owns" the outside (garden, pool, cars, garage), and my areas are the inside of the house (kitchen, bedrooms, living room). I realized my daughter's room was a total mess every day, no matter how I cleaned it. I wanted to use my time more productively and teach her a lesson. I simply "assigned" her the maintenance of the playroom and her room.

Then she didn't want to invite any friends home because "they made a mess," and she also wanted to install a camera to control if someone entered the playroom. I told her that instead of a camera, she should explain to her friends the rules to play in her room before even starting: "you mess up, you clean." And that she should also keep boxes and drawers with labels to make it easier for everyone to clean. BTW, she is only six years old. Get the idea?

Ownership

US Navy seals write in their book Extreme Ownership[18] that "Extreme ownership is the number one characteristic of any high-performing winning team." "We blame our performance on bad luck, circumstances beyond our control, or poorly performing subordinates – anyone but ourselves." Assign maintenance responsibilities to every member of the team and take responsibility for your section. At first, you all will blame others, but you will have to accept the responsibility for failure and find ways to help your team keep your area clean if you want to solve the problem.

I have found it exciting and inspiring that most of the team members in an organization are willing to repair, paint, clean tools, floors, machines, walls, etc. There are many benefits of shining yourself for your area: you can do it the way you really need it. You can do it slowly, without interrupting work. Most of the time, you know exactly what needs to be done and how. And most importantly, you know how to maintain it. Team members get more involved emotionally with the workplace when they have been engaged in the shining process. They feel like real owners. And they start taking maintenance more seriously. Well-implemented cleaning programs have long-term benefits for employee morale and flagging abnormalities.

One of the great things about 5S is that its effects are contagious. During 5S training, I love to tell the story about the trains in New York in the United States. Rudy Giuliani's book "Leadership"[19] talks about how bad the trains and subways in NY used to be. They were usually dirty and deteriorated, which set travelers' mood to fail. As they were dirty, travelers had no respect for them. Graffitis covered subways and buses. Subconsciously, this was alienating people after 2 hours of travel every day seeing this misery. They got frustrated, fussy, and aggressive, probably even contributing to increasing crime issues. The mayor didn't control the Transit Authority, but the mayor was blamed for the graffiti issue.

Giuliani decided to tackle the issue. The whole city, not just the Police Department or the Transportation Department, was involved. Giuliani chose to attack the source by cleaning and painting the trains. They would not let transports run if the graffiti was not cleaned off first. The NYPD would patrol the sanitation areas. Community groups would help to

[18] Jocko Willink and Leif Babin. Extreme Ownership, Hos US navy seals lead and win. St Martin's press, New York. 2015.

[19] Rudolph W. Giuliani. Leadership. 2002.

paint, and they even proposed scratching techniques and new fluids to be more effective.

Usually, after a day of hard work cleaning, they were full of graffiti again the next day. So, his team kept cleaning and painting them again and again. Through time, cleanliness started to last longer. Travelers realized that trains were cleaner, so they were trying harder to respect the rules by not eating inside, cleaning after themselves and throwing trash in the trash cans that were also better maintained. Of course, it wasn't the only change in the city. Still, this one was, for sure, a factor that genuinely impacted travelers' behaviors and sense of psychological safety, not only on the subways but also at their destinations. Millions of workers changed their attitudes when arriving in the city because they traveled in a less hostile, more respectful environment.

Cleaning the facilities and the workplace effectively

This step is about cleaning the facilities and the environment, effectively understanding the need for this task. Effectively means in a way that helps the integral health of the production process in the long term. Cleanliness has different meanings in an operating room, a kitchen or a manufacturing plant. You may not need to meet the same standards for various reasons. But guess who defines the rules? Yes, YOU and YOUR TEAM. The purpose of shine is not to clean more, but to clean better, to better suit our customer and employee needs. Mind the details.

Cleanliness provides a safe work area and makes potential problems visible, e.g., equipment leaks, loose parts, missing guards, paperwork, materials. Sanitation of every place possible includes the ceiling, walls, furniture, drawers, equipment, folders (physical and digital).

Every piece of equipment should have a cleaning checklist. Trash cans should be segregated based on the material they contain to identify rubbish from recycling items.

Maintain the cleanliness achieved with daily work, to maintain the AS-IS standard

Every day, employees should clean the workplace before leaving. There should be a cleaning program, daily, weekly, or monthly.

There must be someone responsible for cleaning, and there must be a responsibility to maintain each of these items. The team can develop two different schedules, one for everyday use and another one for deep expert cleaning. The operator/user can do the superficial cleaning every day (just water). At the same time, there is a kind of SWAT team for a deep cleaning every quarter (water + sanitizer + parts detail cleaning).

Kitchens, operating rooms, or even machines like band saws are examples of areas that cannot wait to be clean "the next week." They need to be cleaned "as you go" to avoid cross-contamination or to avoid getting the dust/debris to spread. Standard pictures, signs or procedures are helpful to instruct the users on maintaining cleanliness (see 4S – Standardize).

Daily maintenance is especially crucial when the object is used/accessed by different users. Some users may not be 5S trained, such as contractors or visitors. 5S visual communication should help everyone to be aligned.

Identify needed tools and products to be able to clean

An essential part of this step that is usually overlooked is identifying the required tools to achieve the normal state of cleanliness. Employees should be able to access the cleaning supplies.

As you can see, 5S is all about making your life easier in the long term. Convenience is key. Sometimes you realize that a standard is not respected just because it is easy to do, or sometimes it is merely not convenient. For example, when there is a lot of trash on the floor, there are no trash cans nearby; they are too small or in an inconvenient spot.

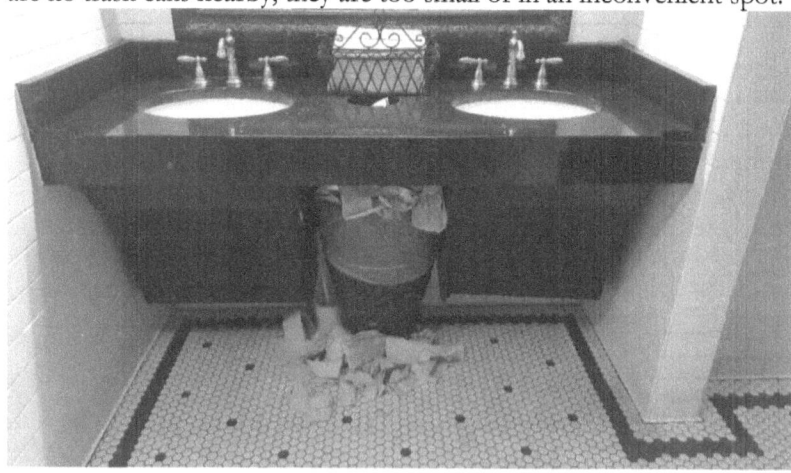

Image 20

There are spots where you already know it will get messy soon, either because the root cause for spills or dust has not been identified/addressed or because it is part of the regular operation. If you look closer to your process, these spots should be easy to locate.

These specific locations can have a particular cleaning station nearby, with all the required elements to clean. The items needed should be well defined, using outlines, a list, or a picture. The inventory includes things like pig mats, mops, cleaners and brushes to complete cleaning according to the standards you set. You may also need special tools like extensions to help you reach high areas or to open compartments.

The cleaning stations should also include a cleaning schedule with the who, what, how, when, and why.

Deliverable microstep #7: Responsibilities for maintenance assigned.

8- Expose complex issues

When one person cleans, she usually gets rid of the visible dust, dirt and debris. This microstep is about focusing on the details. Detailing can take you to expose major problems or inflection points that were acting as barriers to cleanliness.

Cleaning a tube or a measurement device can help you see what the tube contains and read the pressure.

The objective of shine is always to clean better, not more. So, to clean better without spending more time requires that you first identify what is causing the mess in the first place.

Team members sometimes get used to seeing a leak, for example. Probably they reported it a long time ago or even tried to fix it with no luck. In image 21, you can see a leak, but it is simply contained with an old cloth instead of a bucket or solving the leak for good. With the 5S culture, you try your best to expose the leak, analyze it, and solve it immediately (Microstep #9). If it can't be solved, you need to define a process to contain it. If you can't hold it properly (let's say you use a bucket to contain the leak, but it is broken or full!), you don't contribute to shining.

Image 21

Report anomalies

The reason behind the 3rd S is that when a spot is not cleaned or maintained, it probably means hidden problems. Why is it messy in the first place? Is it too difficult to clean? Are there too many leaks? Is there a problem that we have not been able to solve for years? Big issues can come from anywhere, especially from hidden minor issues. 5s takes seriously every single issue, exposes it, and requires a solution to solve it, reduce it, or contain it.

When you define the what, who, when, and how, you usually do it under certain circumstances that you estimate "normal." However, it's frequent that this normal is disturbed by an exceptional circumstance. Turnarounds or temporary changes in personnel or production impact the workflow. It's also very common that during the first year of 5S implementation, cleaning schedules and standards are not fully respected. For example, you are an owner of a sub-section, and you realize the cleaning program has not been signed this week, even though it has been done. Perhaps you found out that not all the parts have been cleaned following the procedure. Whatever is different from expected, it should be recorded or reported. Remember here; the idea is not to blame but to solve. Focus on the solution.

You can use orange cones, signs or tags to expose complex issues. You can also upload the problems to the action plan or the cleaning schedule as a "finding".

Sometimes, the cleaning procedure is not straightforward or feasible, so it should be improved. After successive cleanings, the users should detect the issues themselves and propose to change the procedure. That is where you would start seeing the effects of self-organization. Suggestions for improvement should be notified, updated and resolved shortly to avoid procrastinating about them.

If in doubt, report it out

The cleanliness and organization of a sector are not always your responsibility. Sometimes, you work in other areas that you don't own or go to common areas like bathrooms, kitchens and offices, meeting rooms, and break rooms. But, as mentioned before, your responsibility to clean after yourself never changes; it applies everywhere you go.

In case of not finding an immediate solution, remember you are all connected as part of a process. For example, if you find a leak, trash on the floor, or a machine not working correctly, you need to report it to the owner or the designated responsible.

Now, is there a process in place to report an issue in general? For example, let's say you go to the bathroom in a restaurant and find it all messy and dirty. As a customer, would you report the mess? And as an employee? What is a rule of thumb? Would you clean it or just wait for the designated employee to do it? That's part of the company culture, defined by the procedures and the employees' behaviors.

Most of the restaurants don't ask for help from the customer during the experience. They only ask for feedback when the customer is leaving. Feedback should be as immediate as possible to be impactful. For example, some airports ask for input about restroom cleanliness by asking visitors to push one of two "face buttons" (happy, unhappy – see Image 22). If you decide to have an online reporting process, make sure someone checks and acts to solve complaints; otherwise, nobody will care to use it again.

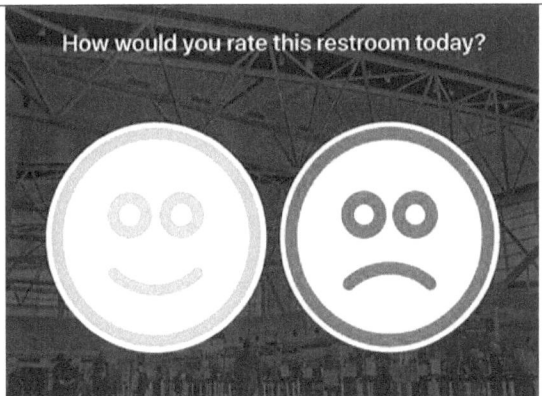

Image 22

Some issues cannot wait, and companies should be aware of that. If your specific workplace is a common area and demands constant attention, make sure there is a means to report issues while you are not available to control them. 5S should be as much self-sustained as possible. Formal reporting allows for better and faster communication of findings company-wide. You can utilize the action plan or the cleaning schedule to report them as action items or observations, provided that they are available in the area.

Identify and map the dirtiest places in your area

Another way to report issues is to "map" them. A map of dirty areas is a diagram showing the sub-section to highlight the different areas in a constant battle with cleanliness.

The idea is to highlight these areas first, prioritize them and plan how to get rid of them, or at least reduce the impact, with the help of the next step #9.

These areas may include oil or water leaks, sources of debris and dirt, hidden or hard-to-reach spots, among others. For example, the floor under a machine, an oven or a fridge is a good spot to hide dirt, food, leaks and missing parts. High ceilings, corners and windows are also common hard-to-reach places.

The map is powerful because it shows, at a glance, all the problems the workplace has. You can update it with red crosses when a new issue arises or a green checkmark when an issue is solved to boost the section morale. It may be helpful to have a laminated map in areas where leaks, dirt, and broken parts are prevalent.

Why do we want to highlight dirty areas?

The main reason to highlight these areas is to do something about them. Remember,

the first step to change is to accept the problem.

It is more effective to do this exercise as a team. If you explore your area, you will probably not notice many issues that a fresh pair of eyes would detect easily. You get used to seeing the problems in such a way that through time, you don't see them anymore, or you simply don't want to fight anymore. "That's the way the company works," you say to yourself. When you learn the 5S culture, you start saying to yourself: NOTHING IS IMPOSSIBLE. This is not the way you want to work; you want to solve this. You can make this work the right way, maybe not today, perhaps not tomorrow, but someday for sure, you will fix it. At least you will start working on it. 5S is all about stopping procrastination and starting to get things done.

Maps

Maps are visual standards of the organization or a specific section to help areas that demand special attention. Focus areas could be areas where no owners are identified or specific systemic issues, like significant amounts of trash, constant leaks, or unsafe conditions. Remote locations, small rooms, storerooms or areas with many pieces of equipment are usually last in 5S implementations. At least with the maps, they can be identified and prioritized. The good thing about tackling these areas is that the improvements are easy to notice and can be used as a 5S marketing strategy within the company. In addition, addressing these areas clearly shows team commitment to the new mindset.

In most companies I worked for, I found hidden areas. I remember a company that was well advanced in 5S. While doing one of the implementation workshops, the employees seemed uncomfortable about a storage room. I wondered what it was and asked them to take me there. It was all dark; the lamp was broken. There were boxes everywhere; you could barely enter. I wondered why nobody had reported it? The employees were really feeling ashamed. I did not blame the employees. They were just following their previous habits of hiding what was wrong. After all the training, they realized something wrong with keeping this room off the radar. They were not able to easily find things there. Nobody was fixing the lamp. It was only more obstacles for them.

The first thing I did was report to the 5S committee meeting that the room had no owner.

It's normal that when you have all organized, and there is one place out of sight, you will try to push all your waste there. It's like a neutral zone where you can "relax." That's why I recommend not to have any grey areas, so that team members avoid the temptation of pushing problems and look for a final solution.

Image 23

5S is systemic, so the idea is not to leave any part out of the equation. However, sometimes areas are left out consciously because the issue is too complex to solve, or sometimes unconsciously because nobody notices it. Usually, leaving a room unattended is that it is too difficult to work with because the employees are not 5S trained or because there is a recurrent root cause. Either way, the best course of action is to keep track of the sub-sections using an area map to see the big picture (systems thinking – CARE value of connecting) and ensure there are no outliers.

Deliverable microstep #8: Complex problems exposed.

9- Prevent small problems from getting bigger

This simple step is one of the keys to the 5S method. The main objective of 5S is to help develop a culture where team members anticipate issues, clean as soon as it gets dirty and, especially, work to ensure cleanliness with the least effort possible.

Every employee needs to be trained to wonder why something gets dirty or why some things often fail and works toward eliminating it, containing or reducing it. Through time, they learn to ask why things are a certain way and how they can change them.

Clean the "hard to clean" places, but, above all, propose ideas to make cleaning easier!

The first microstep was to assign responsibilities. Then the second one was to expose blind spots. Now that you have revealed them, we can't escape from it. The third micro-step in the Shine phase is either to eliminate problems or, at least, make them easier to clean.

How do you make them easier to clean?

To enforce 5S, you shouldn't use coercion, but you should use convenience. For example, locate tools and supplies conveniently, close to where you need them to make it easier to clean.

You can also use devices to help you clean. Some machines have wheels to be able to move them to clean the bottom. Some others have removable pans so that you can easily remove waste. At home, for example, to clean under the bed, buy a mattress that has large legs, and have them exposed so that you can clean it more easily. You can also use devices like the "Roomba" vacuum cleaner to go under the beds, chairs, and sofas easily.

Still, this will only be a reactive approach to the issue. Now, also think about it with a preventive mindset.

Identify the sources of dirt, leaks, dust or any type of disturbances

As mentioned before, team members tend to forget/ignore specific issues reported in the past, but they could not get to solve them.

"I already reported it."

"I know what it is; it can't be done."

"it's too expensive."

Sometimes the issue started many years before them, and the "can't be done" mindset has set a precedent.

Still, the 5S culture in long-term implementations can overcome these barriers and solve the issues for good.

The other frequent problem is that the issues are either too expensive, too difficult to solve, or require a total shutdown.

Let's analyze it first. Everything can be solved if divided into smaller tasks.

Turn problems into smaller and manageable pieces

A deep analysis helps us identify the issue or verify the root cause if it is already well known. It also helps us identify other root causes that may not have been noticed or denoted as irrelevant.

Sticking to the "can't be done" just frustrates the associates. Most of the time, it is true: they did ask for help and didn't get it, it was not a priority, or it was impossible. But focusing on this response doesn't help to get the job done. Instead, a thorough analysis could solve part of the issue that may not be as irrelevant and find alternative solutions that may be easier, more affordable, or at least doable.

On top of this, finding a different response to the same problem has a massive impact on the associate's morale. When team members learn to be part of the solution, they understand the problem's difficulty, and they get to think out of the box. These two factors only help motivate the team, empower them to solve future issues and give them tools to address issues more positively next time. They even work around the problem and solve it by themselves in many cases. It's amazing!! It's worth trying. Always break complex problems into smaller pieces to be able to manage them. Then focus and tackle them individually, one step at a time.

For example, what happens if your car is not working? Would you buy another one, or would you start exploring what's going on? You should start reviewing all the different parts that could be broken, such as lights, battery, oil, gas. If you detect the battery is dead, would you replace it or identify why it is not working? If you keep digging, maybe there is a broken belt, and you only need to replace it. Do you see how much money you can spend with the different options? How much money can you save by taking the time to dig deeper and find the specific problem?

You can perform a root cause analysis with every part that you segregate.

How to Perform a root cause analysis

A root cause analysis will help you brainstorm about the reasons that could trigger your issue. You know the WHAT, WHO, WHEN, HOW, now you will know the WHY.

Various tools can be used to perform a root cause analysis. The most crucial factor is that this thorough analysis is done by the employees working in the section or with the machine under analysis. If they are not involved, the analysis is incomplete. Ideally, the analysis group should be multidisciplinary, including members from different groups such as operations, maintenance, customer service, management, tooling, sales, supply, or procurement, depending on the issue. When you can get a multidisciplinary team of no more than 12 people, you get more ideas, and decision-making is faster to get to a final resolution. See the section (TOOLS TO COMPLEMENT 5S) to learn more about some root causes analysis tools: The 5Why's, FMEA, and Fishbone diagram.

Typical problems:

- Open windows that bring dirt and dust
- Open doors that allow animals to enter
- Water, oil or any other liquid leaking
- Machines, like band saws
- Painting processes
- Manufacturing processes
- Lack of planning
- Rush
- Lack of best practices
- Lack of time to prep the area before working

Take the example of the car. If you had followed the maintenance schedule, would you be surprised b a dead battery? Would you have been able to prevent it?

Make challenging locations easy to clean

Finding time to clean is one of the first challenges. Therefore, it is good to standardize and estimate the time to clean and analyze if the cleaning schedule is doable.

The second challenge is to tackle areas that are difficult to clean.

If cleaning personnel is dedicated to the area, they may or may not have these areas considered or follow the procedure. As a result, they are failing to clean "under the bed." If procedures do not mention clearly that "the floor under the machine/bed has to be cleaned," it is usually not cleaned for long periods. It is your responsibility as the area owner to train someone to take cleaning seriously.

Usually, these difficult locations don't need frequent maintenance. Still, you simply have to define the ideal frequency according to the use. In image 24 below, you can see how a team installed wheels to a small ladder to move it and clean under it.

Management is crucial to revert systemic issues by empowering the team.

Image 24

Deliverable microstep #9: Root causes of dirt reduced.

Implementation Step 3: SHINE

- ✓ Cleaning schedule
- ✓ Training on how to clean
- ✓ Tools needed to clean as required
- ✓ Schedule the time required to do the job
- ✓ Root cause analysis
- ✓ Map of dirty places

Audit Guide 3S

1) There are complete schedules for cleaning everything (what, who, when, how)
2) Team members work in such a way to prevent things from getting dirty
3) Items use covers and devices to facilitate cleanliness
4) There is a specific location to place trash cans and supplies to clean.
5) The places that are hard to access to clean or always dirty are identified and mapped
6) Tools, machines, furniture, equipment and facilities are clean, not oily, dirty or greasy
7) There is a process to identify the root cause for grease, oil, water or dirt and is documented.
8) There is a form to report the cleaning schedule and any anomalies
9) Team members clean immediately after themselves
10) Cleanliness is checked at the end of every shift.

How to practice shining in your day-to-day?

I love the 5S methodology because it helps me reduce my cleaning time. It is a shared responsibility. The only way to achieve a long-lasting clean-up is not to be regularly cleaning but to prevent dirt in the first place by changing small daily habits.

- If you have fewer things, you have fewer things to clean
- If there is constant dirt somewhere, find out the root cause to avoid cleaning in the future. For example, oil, salt and other condiments always seem messy. Place them inside a container to prevent spills. If you eat at your desk, keep a pan or small container to keep the food leftovers from spreading around.
    You can use:

  - carpets to protect the floor
  - table covers to protect the table
  - mats to cover the floor when you paint

- tape to cover wood borders when you paint a wall
- aprons to cover your clothes while you cook
- uniforms to cover your clothes while you work
- pans to contain food packages that may leak

- Keep tools and appliances always clean to ensure they last longer and so that you can also detect when something is wrong. Keeping your fridge clean and organized makes it easier to see when a container is broken, a product is due, or something is leaking.

- Make it convenient for everyone to clean after themselves. Have cleaning sets in different house parts, such as cleansing towels, toilet paper, or brooms. You can also use robots, like the Roomba for the house or the Polaris for the pool, and set them to turn on automatically. For example, locate a trash can next to the dining table to throw away trash right after dinner.

- If you don't use a machine for several days, cover it, for example.
- Performing the tasks can also make it more challenging to clean afterward. Lubrication is a source of oil and mess if it is not done correctly. Identify the best practices, do a single-point instruction, and ensure it is always followed.

These little rules help everyone understand how the house works, and there is no need for you to keep up with everything. A little help from everyone makes it easier to keep the constant flow and avoid stacking plates or clothes by the weekend. All these things are common sense. But are usually used in some circumstances and not in others for no reason. Apply the same thinking to whatever you do, either at home or work, and you will see how your culture changes forever.

Prevention is more important than ever during a massive virus outbreak like the recent COVID-19. Make sure you leave your shoes at the door. Keep a particular location for this close to the door. Clean the cellphone and watch surfaces as soon as you get inside the house or the car. Wash your hands when you are in contact with other people or other surfaces, and keep a hand-sanitizer close to you at all times if you cannot wash your hands.

You may need to develop a new routine and train kids strictly following cleaning routines. For example, if you go to the gym or use shared tools/machines, use disinfecting wipes to clean them before and after use. And last but not least, be mindful when you cough or sneeze, using a tissue or your arm to cover your mouth and nose to avoid other areas getting contaminated, even at home. Germs, viruses and bacteria may remain for a long time on certain surfaces.

5S your mind

Buddhism teaches the importance of cleanliness for having a peaceful mind. Daily tasks like cleaning and cooking are considered spiritual exercises, not different from meditating. Shine helps you appreciate and value what you have today. Be responsible for your life, expose the problems that may blur your happiness and tackle the root cause so that these issues never get back to you—cleanup to welcome success.

Have you found "the best way" to make it shine, and do you need others to follow it? Go to the next Step: Standardize.

Check my Youtube channel for more 5S videos, courses and pictures

https://www.youtube.com/c/lucianapaulise

4S STANDARDIZE

DEFINE A SYSTEM TO MAINTAIN 1S, 2S AND 3S

"In my experience, most troubles and most possibilities for improvement add up to the proportions: 94% belong to the system (responsibility of management), 6% special."

W. Edwards Deming

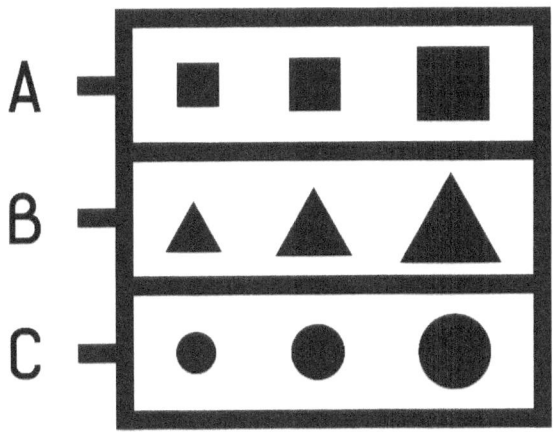

"A key implementation element has been the 5S panel or bulletin board. It quickly reflects the necessary information for programming activities, responsibilities and main results. All personnel involved have followed the project status on the 5S panel. To improve, you must measure, and quick communication of the improvement results can be made using the before and after photo control." In a lab, a team that did not apply 5S committed 20 errors by incorrect use of the equipment versus 5, 3

and 1 errors in the three groups that applied 5S. Two accidents in the first group and no accidents in the other three.[20]

'Seiketsu,' or Japanese for "standardizing," is the fourth step in the 5S process. Now that you know what you need, where to store it and how to maintain it, make it official! This stage builds on the idea of sharing best practices, auditing and checking in on 5S efforts with regularity. By standardizing the approach to 5S, organizational efforts are sustained in the long run by everyone, everywhere.

The step standardize looks forward to finding the best process for each particular task so that sort, store and shine are done consistently by everyone. In this step, you define and communicate routines that help everyone involved to work in sync. What needs to be done, by whom (owner), how (procedure), when (schedule) and why (purpose).

Humans tend to personalize things. "This is my tool, so I know where and how to store it." Still, when you work within an organization, you need to put the team's needs first. I call "We culture" vs. a "Me culture." The first three 5S steps were about individual self-organization, while in the 4th S, you put all the pieces together to self-organize the team and speak in terms of "we," not just "me."

During this phase, there will be responsibilities as an individual and responsibilities working in a team:

- Develop visual aids and standards to help to keep the workplace organized and clean with clear directions
- Learn to work using procedures, not only yours but also the ones of the places you go to
- Learn to prepare, write, read and improve procedures
- Learn the importance of respecting the rules everywhere you are
- Understand the importance of each of the functions in your organization. When you don't commit to your duty, you are impacting others.

---

[20] 5S methodology implementation in the laboratories of an industrial engineering university school Mariano Jiménez (a), Luis Romero (b), Manuel Domínguez (b), María del Mar Espinosa (b). a) Department of Mechanical Engineering, Technical School of Engineering – ICAI, Universidad de Comillas, Madrid, Spain. b) Design Engineering Area – Universidad Nacional de Educación a Distancia (UNED), Madrid, Spain

5S efforts should be challenged regularly by any team member. Whenever a problem is exposed, consider asking the following:

- Is there a standard to do the task?
- If there is a standard, is it being followed?
- Is the standard correct or updated?

You will need to define standards, establish schedules, and engage the workforce, showing the rules all around the workplace. Behaviors and habits are more natural to acquire if the context always tells us what to do.

The three microsteps to implement the standardize phase are:

10) Define the rules for self-organization
11) Make the rules visible and available
12) Practice and communicate continuously

10- Define the rules for self-organization

As you will read in the section ACHIEVING CULTURAL CHANGE, defining a purpose and clear values is crucial for a long-term shift to self-organization. Therefore, it is good to set simple behavioral rules during 5S implementation. They should be easy to copy by observation and imitation.

Generation X and Baby boomers will probably follow the rules just because they are being told. Still, as of 2020, 40% of the workforces are either Millennial or Gen Z, and they will not follow instructions not being engaged unless they know why.

Values can be already defined at the company level or specially designed for the project, but they have to be embraced and respected by everyone.

In 5S implementations, teamwork is essential. The "me" mindset should shift to a "we" mindset. When you are implementing 5S, you are not only implementing a 5S culture but a "We Culture," with behaviors focused on the benefit of the team. A clear purpose of a "we culture" is to care for your teammates and workplace. Why is caring so important?

When you ask team members why they think the workplace is not in good shape, they usually say "because the other team members don't care." It's often the main root cause, so you need to focus on training them to care for others to allow team engagement and self-organization.

CARE can be translated into four values: connect, attend, respect and empower.

1. Connect your purpose to your team's purpose. The company's goals, values, and long-term objectives are well-known and shared with everyone. You know how your minor changes and self-organization impact others.
2. Attend actively: Employees are encouraged to follow up metrics, understand results and use data to make decisions. Attention to detail and changes in the environment is key to reacting quickly and adapting.

3. Respect diversity and improve psychological safety: Promoted collaboration, knowledge sharing, communication, and teamwork. Team members are encouraged to respect each other and even respect things. Interactions are continuous.
4. Empower others and learn self-discipline: There are formal processes to expose tasks, actions and results to increase autonomy and self-discipline. Team members decide how to perform their work.

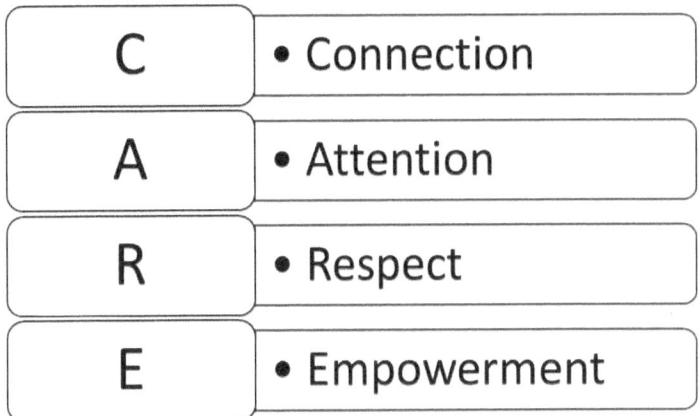

C	• Connection
A	• Attention
R	• Respect
E	• Empowerment

These values help employees understand the 5S steps much better. You need to learn 5S because you are part of a system; everything you do impact other processes. 5S helps you self-organize to work better in teams (team members are connected).

You define the home for a tool or write down a standard so that others can work autonomously (team members are empowered with the knowledge). You store the instrument in its place to respect the other employees that may use it later on (team members are respected). You ask yourself why an item is stored in a particular place when it would be more efficient to store it somewhere, therefore propose a change in your action plan.

Respect, in particular, is one of the most important values that 5S represents. Respect yourself, your team, the rules defined by everyone, and the things you use to work (tools, floor, equipment etc.) as if they all were one. That's why you follow the third principle, "look like brand-new."

Training sessions, audits and team meetings should always remind these values (or the ones chosen by the company) to engage the team members. That's why the 4S standardize is essential.

The team becomes the center of the action and decisions. A diamond-like structure replaces the typical pyramid of the hierarchy, as shown in image 25. Leaders set the purpose and support the efforts, customers are at the top telling the team what their priorities are, and the team defines how to get things done.

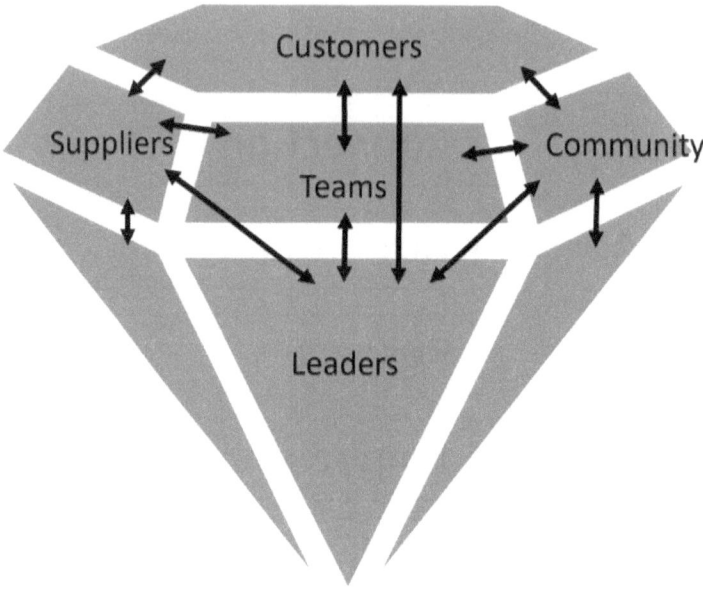

Image 25

Involve the whole team

All the team members need to carry out the cleaning of the sector. All the team members need to be involved in asking and answering the following questions:

a) WHAT needs to be cleaned?

Register in a file or a checklist all the items that need to be cleaned regularly: Machines, walls, ceilings, doors, floors, windows, glass, mirrors, pipes, tools, tables etc. When we do this, we may realize that some items are easy to clean, others that are more difficult, some that are usually kept clean, some that often get super dirty. We will need to define and assign priority, frequency, and quality standards to clean all these items based on time availability and its impact on the customer or our teammates. Remember, the purpose of all this 5S effort is to ensure a better environment to work for a team to build the best product for the customer. That's why we need the user to decide what to clean. Usually, the user is the most knowledgeable. Nor the leader or the manager. They will only assign resources to help us make better decisions.

If the place presents specific issues or problems, just go to the next microsteps 8) and 9).

b)   WHO needs to clean it?

Who performs the task should be decided as a team, considering who is the best suited for the work and the resources available. The job owner can be an external company or the very user; it just depends on the nature of the item, the required frequency, the required knowledge. You may need an expert to come at specific periods for particular machines while the operators do daily maintenance. When possible, tasks can be rotated among all the employees in the section to ensure that everyone understands the importance of the task, respects its rules, and evaluates its effectiveness. This way, everything is part of our job; nobody can say, "it is not my job."

c)   WHEN is the best time to ensure effectiveness?

To decide when the team needs to be as specific as possible: the day of the week, shift, time, etc. We may need different timings for the same item for different purposes. Sometimes it is just a simple dust cleaning versus a deep cleaning at the end of the month or during a turnaround.

d)   HOW is the best way to clean it?

Assign the task to clean a table to two different people. How did they clean it? Did they clean it the same way? How was the top cleaned? Did they clean the legs? Which supplies were used, were they different? Different people have different ways of cleaning based on previous experiences, based on what they consider important and the time they decide to dedicate. The HOW needs to be as specific as possible to ensure standardization across the team.

e)   WHY is it dirty?

It is also very important to determine the nature of the source of dirt. Is it dirty because of the regular usage of the item? For example, a bandsaw will always create a mess of debris and dust after it is used. For any object, we need to start thinking if there is a way to avoid the mess at all, reduce it, or at least contain it, as discussed in 3S – Shine. If we don't think before cleaning, we may be spending more time cleaning than working, and we can't allow that to happen. It is all about cost-benefit. Through 5S, we should set a new level of cleanliness, as we dedicate less effort to cleaning while we improve cleanliness. If we slowly get rid of all the sources of issues, cleaning will be a lot easier. Working as "an operating room" will not be just a dream but a reality.

Cleaning and maintenance schedules:

A cleaning schedule is a plan for carrying out the cleaning or maintenance process. It includes WHAT needs to be done, WHO will do it, WHEN and HOW. See tables 1, 2 and 3.

Schedules need to be designed by the users of each section. A model can be applied, but the user needs to develop the specific methods, frequency, supplies, etc.

SECTION: WAREHOUSE	METHOD	FREQUENCY	DAYS	WHO	ELEMENTS	SPECIFICATIONS	STANDARD
Eliminate dust from the shelves	dry	3 times x week	Mo. We. Fr	A	Cotton	Wipe clean with cotton waste. Start by cleaning the upper level, continue...	No oil and dirt
Clean the furniture							
Clean corners							
Clean ventilations							
Clean walls and ceilings							
Vacuum the floor							

Image 26

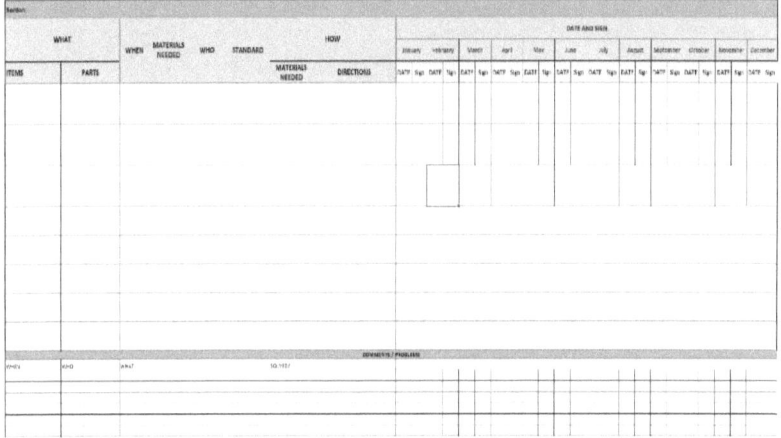

Image 27

Lubrication		Location:		Code:	
Machine:		Area:		Frequency (days)	
Supplier:		Location:		1	
Model:		Hr of maintenance per year:			
Herramientas y Materiales		**Machine Expert:**		**Operator position**	
				?	
		Lubricants		**Machine condition**	
Full Diagram		**Report**			
		# points to be lubricated			
		Average time per point (min):			
		Total time (min):			
		Detailed diagrams			
SAFETY EQUIPMENT NEEDED					
WORK INSTRUCTIONS					

Image 28

Some things to include in cleaning schedules:
1) Map of the area or sub-section
2) Owner
4) List the items to be cleaned by each sub-section
    a. Machines
    b. equipment
    c. Transportation
    d. Tools
    e.Lightening
    e. Facilities
        i. Ceilings
        ii. Pipes
        iii. Cable trays
        iv. Walls
        v. Floors

5) Each sub-sector will have its cleaning routine:
   a. Items (what)
   b. How
   c. When
   d. Who
6) Places of difficult access
7) Root Causes and their solution
8) Anomalies detected and observations (only to fill in when there are exceptions to the process)
9) Map of leaks and dirty places.
10) Record of work done, such as employee signature or date of completion.
11) Pictures showing the standard that wants to be maintained.

The importance of routines, even in hard times

Rudy Giuliani said in his book *Leadership*, "One might suppose that attending to the details would assume less importance during times of crisis, but the reverse is true." In times of crisis, standards start to be overlooked for some reason, when they should be more critical than ever. Following rules and routines during a crisis help us to get ordinary things done and focus our attention on new challenges.

Routines help us follow a common thread when we feel lost or uncertain. That's why seniors like to stick to a simple routine once they stop working. They want to wake up, receive calls from their grandkids, or go for a walk, always at the same time. Waiting for the same to happen the next day helps them overcome solitude or boredom. Kids also appreciate routines. The first thing we all learn when having a baby is to keep a schedule for eating and sleeping.

If the what, when, who, where, and why are overlooked just because they seem obvious, 5S starts failing long-term. For example, if you don't choose in advance the best moment to do the job, it is more likely that you will forget to do it or skip it. Every new habit you learn with 5S is just like exercising or running. If you don't add it to your routine, it's hard to keep it.

Let's say it has to be done on Monday; which shift will do it? If it is not defined, both shifts will push it or spend time discussing it every time. So why don't you just standardize it?

My husband loves running, but he would struggle to find some time to run between work and the house chores. He would always find reasons to change his schedule, making running a second priority. I insisted that he keep a program that was convenient for him and the family and stick to it so that his body would adapt. He said the perfect time was 6 AM, but he couldn't have breakfast so early and started running right away. I insisted that if he practiced running without having breakfast, his body would get used to it after the first week. And he did. Defining a schedule made it much easier for him to just wake up instead of making a decision every morning. He was able to run the NY Marathon soon after changing his routine without feeling guilty or stressed. Small details can change our lives in ways we can't even imagine.

We need to establish formally the rules proposed in the previous steps so that they are clear for everyone by using:
- ✓ Procedures
- ✓ Checklists
- ✓ Pictures
- ✓ Schedules
- ✓ Diagrams
- ✓ Shadows
- ✓ And anything that the team members can think of to make it easy and convenient to follow the procedures.

Tips for creating procedures
If procedures are not simple and conveniently located, they are ineffective. Procedures must:
- Be easy to read and understand
- Include Visual Communication (graphics, photos, etc.)
- Include defined Visual Control (the shine definition is clearly shown through pictures or diagrams)
- Include Control Record
- Include a communication plan to all members of the sector, with a defined training record
- Be located in the place where they are required

Deliverable microstep #10: Standards defined

11-   Make the rules visible and available

A 5S workplace should be easily recognized by its visual communication (labels, colors, shading and poka-yoke gadgets). Interactions within self-organized systems are based on both signals and cues derived from the environment, work in progress, and fellow workers. These signals need to be simple to allow team members to adapt quickly.

We have many sensors in our bodies: smell, touch, vision, hearing. They give us clues about what we need to focus on. Although the term "visual control" is used, the implemented controls often relate to the other senses (hearing, touch, smell, and taste).

Most companies today already have procedures for their most important tasks. But for some reason, when you watch employees doing their jobs, each employee does it differently most of the time. Be encouraged to ask about specific details of the task, such as the correct size for the x-gauge, and they are unsure. Each employee responds with a different answer. Why does this happen? What about the standard?

The rules tend to be slightly modified over time. For example, when you try to remember a movie, some details are blurred in your mind. When you do the same activity, you adapt the procedure for your convenience, almost by accident. Changing the procedure for convenience can be a great idea, but why not make it official?

It's just that procedures aren't usually stored near where the work is done. They are probably in a large folder inside the office, on a shared disk or, unfortunately, were sent to external storage. And if they are available, updating them is usually not an "employee-friendly" practice. Maybe a consultant does it three years later when it's time to update the ISO.

Generally, employees are not empowered to review or update the rules daily. Even so, processes are permanently changed by employees on an informal basis. It doesn't make sense. It makes perfect sense. Employees, over time, understand the tips and tricks of their process. Have you seen a baby eating? Through practice, they learn how to eat, use their hands more effectively to get more food in less time, order food, and throw food away to complain. It's part of their development.

The practice is part of employee development as well. As they become experts in a process, they must be empowered to communicate their improvements constructively.

What is the point of these manuals if you cannot read or update them at any given time, and should they not be available, especially to new hires?

It's all about convenience.

Make it convenient to find, easy to follow and easy to update.

The procedures and rules do not have to be a heavy and complex manual to be good.

You can save the massive manual and then simply have pocket editions or more visual versions on the workstations.

It is necessary to facilitate compliance by making the standards visible to everyone on the workstation and available for easy retrieval.

Tips
Some procedures, such as in the automotive or health industry, must be followed to the letter and cannot be changed for convenience unless the change is approved. Other sectors, such as the service industry, may not be as strict. For example, some *call centers* no longer require scripts. In any case, the company needs to clearly define if processes can be changed and how the changes should be standardized. So, yes, we need a procedure on how to build procedures! We'll look at this in more detail in microstep #12 to learn more about this.

The following are all ways to help maintain a standard.
a) Checklists
b) Images
c) Photos
d) Diagrams
e) Signage
f) Job aids
g) Positioning Markers
h) Arrows
i) The signs that change with changing conditions
j) Containers or drawers that indicate the size
k) Poka-yoke devices (see TOOLS FOR THE 5S COMPLEMENT - Poka-yoke)

l)   Flow charts

m)   Tables

Job aids are any sheets or instructions in the area or workstation that help the operator or the team do their work or train others to do the work. They may include

- Quality control points and descriptions
- Images or diagrams of the processes
- Workspace flowcharts.
- Pictorial explanations of the work to be done
- The highlights of the most common mistakes

Transparency is a fundamental value in team communication

The goal is to make it easier to determine when something needs to be done, either because it is part of the process or something unusual that needs to be fixed. Every day, some things need to be done: refill, repair a machine due to a malfunction, fix a mistake or approve. The key here is to understand that it is okay to identify errors or problems; it is NOT okay to hide them or avoid reporting them.

It is part of a thriving 5S culture to expose problems to solve them as soon as possible. The easier they are detected, the easier it is for the team to self-organize to solve them. Transparency is a fundamental value to help teams work effectively and build trust.

Use visual and audible aids to maintain standards and define levels of acceptability/assistance/functions

The use of visual and hearing aids is as important as the performance of the procedures. If you don't see it or hear it, it doesn't exist, right? This step is about having it at hand and making it easier for everyone around you to detect errors and follow the procedures. It is advantageous when different people have access to the section, such as contractors, suppliers or customers, who are probably not trained in 5S. It is necessary to help them "see" what they need to do as part of their job. Cleaning is also part of their job; not being employed does not exclude them from finishing their tasks.

Audible aids

Japanese train drivers practice *shisa kanko* ("check and call"), pointing out what they need to check and then naming it out loud (even if they are alone!). It is a mistake prevention exercise that railway employees have used for more than 100 years. It's a dialogue with themselves to make sure nothing is overlooked. When asked to perform a simple task, workers typically make 2.38 mistakes for every 100 actions. When *shisa kanko* is used, this number drops to just 0.38 - a massive 85% improvement, according to the BBC article "Japanese skill copied by the world."[21]

When forklifts are going in reverse, they automatically turn on a siren or alarm to prevent other employees from walking around.

At Toyota plants, they use what they call an Andon to alert when there is a problem on the production line. Any problem or deviation from the standard, regardless of size or severity, is exposed. A cable over the workstation activates a warning light or audio alarm, usually soft music. It alerts team leaders to provide support.

For example, in a hospital, there are various hearing controls, such as medical equipment alarms and other electrical devices or ventilation systems.

Visual management

Communication is not always easy; more than 60% of communication occurs in a non-verbal way in a chat with someone, for example. That's why adding a visual part to the verbal part helps clarify.

For example, using colored tubes and keeping them clean is one way of communicating.

A uniform is a type of visual communication to describe people's roles to other employees and the end consumers. For example, when you go shopping and visit a store, uniforms help you know who the manager or salesperson is. Everything can be easily identified with the right tools:

- Oil level: when should we fill more oil?
- Level of responsibility: Who is the designer of the space?
- Efficiency: Are we efficient, or do we need to improve?
- Storage location: Is this the right place to store this product?
- Dangerous areas: can we go in, or should we take precautions?
- Status of the process: What is left to finish?
- Runners: Where can I walk?

---

[21] http://www.bbc.com/travel/story/20170504-the-japanese-skill-copied-by-the-world

- Emergency exits: Where should I exit?

It's also great to identify items that are out of service or containers that need to be refilled. How can you go to a bathroom in a remote location without even speaking the language? Usually, you'll find signs that are understood globally.

Image 29

Visual controls
Visual checks communicate information so that activities must be carried out according to the rules. For example, painted aisles, machine guards, color-coded lubrication inlets direct and control specific human behaviors.

For example, a safety instruction may say: "Stand at one foot of the control panel." Not all countries understand distance in terms of feet; some use meters. A visual clarification and reminder such as a tape marking the safe area help to align communication.

Of course, you shouldn't abuse visual controls by putting too many in one place, or you'll make people ignore them completely. You need to prioritize. To establish adequate visual controls, you need to ask yourself:

- What do you want to control?
- What are the critical points?

- What constitutes an abnormality?
- What are the rules?
- Is the problem easy to solve?
- What tools are used for inspection?
- Is the inspection easy?
- What are the emergency procedures?

It is important to understand the differences between simple visualization and visual control to choose the most effective tool needed in a given situation. In some cases, a problem can be solved simply by sharing information through visualizations. In other cases, a visual check will be needed to maintain on-site control of work activities.

Visual checks are used to: develop standards, alert us to abnormalities and speed up recovery, stop defects or prevent them from continuing and directly prevent faults from occurring through poka-yoke (error-proof) systems.

Image 30

Visual control is the type of control that allows anyone, even unfamiliar with the work area, to recognize important information, what needs to be done (e.g., filling out an inventory), and identify problems, waste, or deviations from standards.

In image 30, you are expected to refill the bucket when the material reaches the red mark. Likewise, in image 31, you are expected to review the stock when you see a red square instead of a green one.

Image 31

You have to be very smart and make it visually easy for people to know what's coming next.

The example below shows four different options for keeping a meter under control:

a) Read a meter against a control sheet or standard worksheet.
b) Read the standard indicated on cards or stickers.

c) See the standard stated on the meter (see picture below, standard value marked in blue on the meter).

d) See the warning signal; a buzzer or light gets activated when there is a problem

Which one do you think is more useful in keeping everyone involved? Check image 32 below.

Image 32

What can you identify visually?

There are specific places where you can start working:

- Locating central storage areas
- Locate safety showers and fire extinguishers
- Locate the exits and the bathrooms
- Determine the minimum and maximum inventory levels for each storage area
- Locate the location of each item (2nd S - Sectorize)
- Locate a breakdown sequencing area within each central storage area.
- Determine appropriate storage methods for each part.
- Locate minimum and maximum inventory levels.
- Locate areas for idle material handling devices.
- Locate areas for replacement equipment or parts
- Material flow shelves.
- Material indicator lights.

- Full/empty marks on a container
- Full/empty refueling card.
- Machines on / off.
- Locate parking space for devices such as forklifts when not in use
- Mark or color-code the floor to take advantage of the space: safe aisles, defective parts, waste, various types of garbage, tooling installation, change areas, quality control, employee rest areas, cart location, trash location, and machine location.
- Mark the status of a process. Some examples of these labels include red labels (to sort out unnecessary items), Quality Feedback System labels, waste labels, defect labels, hold labels, refill labels, hazardous, controlled. You can update the label with the date, responsible and the date of the next check.

Displaying programs and schedules

The best way to help everyone respect them for lengthy procedures is to check off the steps on a list each time the task is performed. Lists are good for ensuring tasks are done regularly and clear responsibilities. In addition, they help you understand which steps to consider for the task at hand and act as reminders of what needs to be done and in what specific order.

Although 5S responsibilities must be assigned to a single person at a specific time to avoid confusion or gray areas, everyone is collectively responsible for the outcome. We can all check if the tasks are being performed or need more attention.

Restaurants tend to display their cleaning schedule to push control not only to employees but also to customers. If done correctly, it is also a marketing strategy to show cleanliness and care.

Before and after pictures:

Before and after images are visual standards (see image 33) that remind users how the item looked before and after applying 5s. It consists of two photos: one when the action item is open and the second when it is closed and the problem is solved. It is unnecessary to have a before and after photo for each enhanced element. Indeed you have to prioritize in which cases a photo helps users understand the standard. These images are instrumental in common areas, such as meeting rooms or tool rooms. The goal is to be striking, showing users how they should behave. Sometimes it is difficult to set a standard for all items. A picture is worth a thousand words.

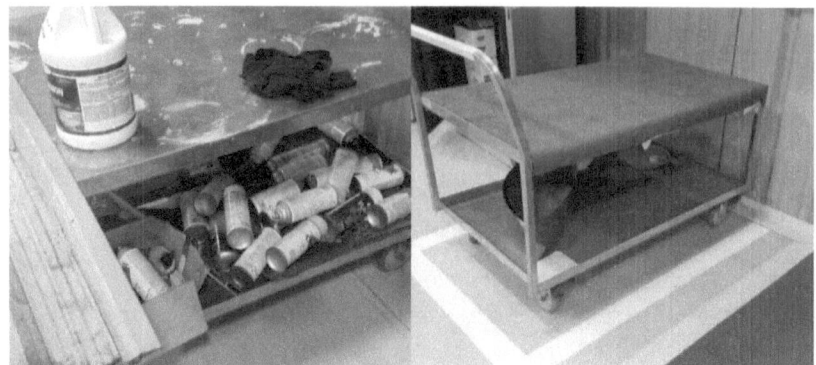

Image 33 - Before and after image

Deliverable microstep #11: Procedures and standards visible and available

12-   Communicate continuously

Once the best practices have been defined, agreed and exposed, you must ensure everyone knows about them. New habits emerge from multiple interactions among the team members reacting to changes in the environment.

Communicate everyone involved in the change

Team meetings (5S CONCEPTS – Team Routines) are excellent ways to share updated procedures and standards. For the sake of the process, communicate the changes to everyone involved: employees, contractors, customers or suppliers.

Communication channels:

- Single Point Lessons are critical because they provide maintenance information on what to do, how to do it, and why it should be done.
- Improvement bulletins show changes in equipment maintenance procedures.
- Tags and diagrams are also handy because they make identifying problems, locating utilities, and performing tasks easier.
- Visual reaction plans show how to respond to problems effectively.
- Status boards on docks enable the logistics provider to deliver materials to the closest point of use or storage area, thereby minimizing material handling activities and material movement.
- Identification Stickers can be used in several ways to help visually control the work area and help all employees understand when something has deviated from its standard. Here are some examples of how stickers and markings can be used: direction of flow, the direction of knob rotation, appropriate fluid level, acceptable gage range, On/off positions.
- Work Group Display Boards can be used for communication purposes among all employees within a Work Group. They can be used to communicate 5s audit results, safety information and statistics, Production levels, defects levels, Pareto diagrams, Minutes from standup meetings, awards and employee announcements.
- Newsletters, emails, intranets and team chats are good to communicate cross-functional processes

- Face-to-face meetings and coaching sessions
- Virtual meetings
- Pictures of before and after

Have a process in place for updating procedures in case of process change

Whenever there is a standard, no matter the format (a picture, a checklist or a manual), it becomes a living document, meaning that it can change through time. There must be a process to update processes. Changes need to be communicated, and old procedures stored as past versions in case there are audits or recalls in the future.

What could change?

Anything can change. New team members, new machines added, new products, new tools.

I have seen cases where 5S is sustained until there is a significant change and the group doesn't know how to deal with it, so simply get back to the old habits. Sometimes it is merely a tough month with many orders in place to manufacture, forcing employees to reduce the cleaning schedule.

In one of the companies I worked for, employees have developed a process to restock inventory on their workstations. To reduce inventory, the company changed the procedure to avoid employees keeping a stock of gloves and other consumables in their workstations; the leader had to keep the stock. This process reduced the inventory but also the efficiency and flow of the process, sometimes delaying lead time. The employees were not comfortable, but they didn't speak. The change was noticeable when I audited them, as their little tool shelves were empty. We discussed ways to improve the new procedure to ensure the flow of the process, still keeping the inventory low. We also reviewed how they could have new visual standards, as the previous ones they have created were useless.

Team members need to learn to adapt and update processes when required. If there is a new item on stock, the inventory list needs to be updated. If there are new team members, schedules and area owners need to be updated.

Changes need to be communicated the right way. Communicating and approving changes varies from company to company, but the essential part is to review the proposed amendment with the process owners and other employees or customers impacted.

Some things to consider:

- Contact everyone involved (employees, leaders, other departments, customers, suppliers, contractors)
- Ask for input from internal or external customers and suppliers as needed, involve them in the solution
- Make sure the change is good for the system as a whole, not only for one department to the detriment of others
- Define a change management process (includes communication, training everyone involved and monitoring the change)

Communicating changes in office or remote work

In manufacturing, a change in a process may be noticeable. At the same time, in an office environment, where everyone has their computers or even working remotely, it is very common to change processes unilaterally. You take a new task, you don't understand why you need to send a specific report, so you don't send it anymore, or you just change the format to make it easier for you. Before doing it, you should consult the customer, the person who is receiving the report, to see if the changes impact their work or not. Sometimes what makes it easier for you to make it difficult for others. Simply make sure the total workflow result is improved or not impacted negatively. Sometimes it makes it difficult for others, but the result for the end customer is better, or control is improved, so it may make sense anyway to implement it. Again, first thing first, review it as a team and get ready to expose the pros and cons before making any changes.

Have a process in place for training new hires or employees taking new positions

Procedures change over time, due to external reasons or as part of a continuous improvement effort. Sometimes, procedures change just because someone new gets into the loop not adequately trained. Changing positions is now more often than ever. Standardized processes ensure better transitions as long as new employees are informed. The onboarding process is key to ensuring rules, values, and standards are communicated from the very beginning. Knowledge helps to empower employees to make their own decisions and prevent management from micro-managing, especially in self-organized companies.

Deliverable microstep #12: Rules 100% communicated and implemented.

Implementation Step 4: STANDARDIZE

✓ Review the implementation of the 3s and review what standards need to be created

✓ Define the rules for organization and cleanliness

✓ Procedures and standards should be visible and available

✓ Use visual and audible aids to communicate the agreements continuously

✓ Implement the standards

Audit Guide 4S

1) There are procedures to carry on the main 5S activities, like cleaning, storing or labeling
2) Procedures and rules are updated, communicated accordingly and easy to access
3) The shine definition is clearly shown through pictures or diagrams)
4) The 5S action plan is updated systematically by everyone in the area
5) There are visual controls for the main required activities in the area
6) All the machines and equipment have a preventive maintenance schedule
7) Maintenance schedules are registered or logged for the record
8) The methodology and updates are communicated systematically to everyone in the company
9) Teams use boards to share date and procedures
10) There is a system to continue training team members, leaders, new members and suppliers on 5S

How to practice standardizing in your day-to-day?

Routines, standards and procedures are helpful whenever you have to do something repetitively or something is used/accessed by different people. They help you do it more effectively following the best practice and help everyone do it the same way.

Everything can be standardized, from where you store your dirty clothes to your car keys or how you make breakfast. If most of the little things that you do every day are done in a standardized way, repetitively by mindfully, you can get them done faster.

Standardization helps me to solve those small little daily things. For example, I love drinking my sparkling water cans cold. So every time I refill the cans shelf in the fridge, I start on the right side, so I always get the cold ones on the left. The golden rule: never have less than three. Restock on three because it takes me around half day to drink three, and it is the time the water needs to get cold.

Define cleaning schedules for every family member. Everyone has different expectations of their home organization, so setting standards help to stop assuming. Then, agree with the house members on how to get things done.

There are tons of poka-yoke tools that you can use, like a dishwasher visual sign showing if it contains clean or dirty plates—no reason to fight.

Take pictures of before and after (imagine how your garage could look free of clutter), and define cleanliness standards (what is accepted and what is not).

Colors can help you store by the due date or remind you when to re-stock. That way, anyone can be responsible for shopping. Pictures, signs, transparent containers; everything is welcome to make it easier for everyone to understand the rules of the house. Standardization is key to avoiding miscommunication.

Image 34

5S your mind

Pandemics, virus outbreaks and global threats will be more common. In the case of the 2020 COVID-19 outbreak, doctors recommended cleaning your hands more often, practicing social distance and being more careful when touching a surface to reduce the odds of getting in touch with the virus. If you experienced it, you probably came to realize that there are many things that you were taking for granted that you didn't even think about during the day. Perhaps you didn't notice that you were touching your face so often. Maybe you thought you didn't need to care about cleanliness because a janitor or maid would clean later for you.

When implementing the 5S culture, this is business as usual. It is just like practicing mindfulness in every action. You have to do it consciously in every task or activity, not in auto-pilot mode. That's the only way to follow the agreed standards and avoid leaving issues unattended.

Practicing a state of working with care and present awareness helps significantly reduce accidents and mistakes and increase satisfaction at work.[22]

Productivity is also about increasing satisfaction at work because you have more time for doing the things you love! Free time is a matter of strategy and standards! Commit to following through with your plans and best practices, trust the process and move on.

Have you defined standards, but you and your team fail to sustain them through time? Then, go to the next Step: Self-organization.

Download the We Culture app for more free resources and training courses

www.theweculture.com

---

[22]https://www.psychologytoday.com/us/blog/urban-survival/201810/new-research-suggests-mindfulness-improves-job-satisfaction

5S SELF-ORGANIZE

MAKE 5S PART OF YOUR DAY-TO-DAY

"Do the right thing even when nobody is looking"

(Continuous from the introduction). During the pilot test, team members found it easier to sort and find items in sections where there is full 5S compliance.

"When it was not fully adhered to, not all shelves were labeled, or items were not properly cleaned before storing. When they were retrieved for reuse, they needed to be cleaned again, thereby adding to the time delay. The "Shine" aspect was being partially implemented. There were no documented work methods and so there were variations in time taken to sort and find items. The "Standardized" procedures were lacking. Due to the partial- and non-compliance of the above aspects of 5S, the last aspect, "Sustain" (self-organize) could not yet be considered in the current situation. This is because the first four aspects needed to be fully implemented before the sustain aspect can be initiated.

The experiment showed that throughput increased by approximately 40% when normal sort time was reduced by about 80% implementing 5S."[23]

---

[23] "The implementation of 5S lean tool using system dynamics approach" 27th CIRP Design 2017 Oleghe Omogbai and Konstantinos Salonitisa

In Japanese, sustaining self-organization, or "shitsuke" is the fifth and most challenging step in the 5S process. It means training and self-disciplining the team to achieve self-organization over time, even when no one is in control.

Self-organization is also called spontaneous order and can be found in different fields naturally, as in

- physics, spontaneous magnetization
- chemistry, in the molecular self-assembly
- Biology, in social behaviors such as bees, ants, fish and termites
- IT, in the optimization algorithms

A colony of thousand termites self-organizes to build a nest. Workers rely on information from the environment, work-in-progress, and multiple interactions among their partners.

In the beginning, not much seems to get done. Over time, however, a pattern appears, a snowballing effect of positive feedback takes control, and termites build where there is already some building[24].

These examples suggest that self-organization can be used in human society, especially to solve complex issues, such as in a company.

The ultimate goal is to help people become more autonomous, including working remotely. Each member of the organization must know what to do, how, where, when and why. When employees organize themselves, cleaning and organizing become part of their daily work.

Self-auditing your sections, finding ways to improve your processes and setting your own goals also becomes part of your daily work. It is under these conditions that 5S can be sustained over time.

That's why the 5th S Self-organization is the most difficult of the five steps, and not all companies reach this stage. Human beings are always resistant to change. We all resist changing our habits and acquiring new ones. When one tries to change a deep-rooted habit, one is usually tempted to return to that habit without even noticing it. One becomes

---

[24] Self-Organization in Biological systems. Scott Camazine, Jean-Louis Deneubourg, Nigel R. Franks, James Sneyd, Guy Theraulaz and Eric Bonabeau. Princeton University Press. 2001.

convinced that it is part of one's personality by saying, for example, "I am not one of those who get up early. However, habits depend on you; they are not part of the genetic information. It requires effort and teamwork more than anything else. Remember, you are not lazy; you just want to save energy. But with 5S, you can save even more and enjoy it most of all!

Now, let's go over the steps of the 5S, the four values and the three principles (remember 5x4x3):

5 steps:

- Sort
- Store
- Shine
- Standardize
- Self-organize

4 Values:

- Connection
- Attention
- Respect
- Empowerment

3 Principles

- "A home for everything and everything in its home. "
- "Everything is found in less than 30 seconds."
- "Everything looks brand new."

The problem now is how to implement them in your daily life.

Change is not easy. As mentioned in the case of the introduction to the chapter, partial compliance with rules and agreements means that the final result is not as exponential as expected. That is why sustaining new habits is the key to successfully implementing 5S.

Iterate continuously without fear of failure

The key to being more adaptable to change in agile systems is learning to iterate. Ideas are welcome as the only means of moving forward. Team members are trained to observe the environment and propose ideas on better adapting to it. The preconception is that ideas are all good; some may work better than others or be more necessary because nothing is called failure. Each test is part of a learning curve, like in the book's introduction. The continuous cycle is similar to observing, testing, and improving the Introduction: repeat the current process and observe any environmental disruptions or potential obstacles. Once you master it, make micro changes to make it better. This cycle is the key to self-organization. See image 35.

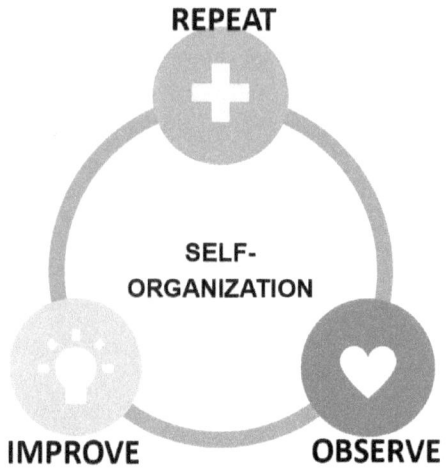

Image 35: Self-organizing culture

The key is in the last three microsteps:

13) Repeat, repeat and repeat

14) Observe the current process to remove obstacles

15) Make micro-changes continuously to improve

13- Repeat, Repeat and Repeat

You've learned to see with a different lens; you've learned to talk when you think something smells funny; you've learned to meet standards. Now all you have to do is keep repeating everything you have learned. You have to be present and attentive as you work, watching what is happening wherever you are and looking for how to best collaborate for the common purpose.

The problem we often encounter, especially with young or entry-level workers, is that they do not always perform as expected, no matter how easy the job is. They have too many ups and downs in the way they work. One day they are "employee of the month," the next day, they don't even show up for work. And in most cases, they like the job, and they are willing to do it. Still, sometimes they can be rude to customers, arrive late or interrupt the status quo for no apparent reason. That is when leaders usually come into play and "micro-manage" them by controlling every step and telling them what to do, punishing them or doing the work for them. None of these solutions work in the long term. They are only short-term solutions that do not address the root cause.

Usually, employees do not perform as expected because they lack the self-discipline to maintain a routine work schedule. Self-discipline has a more significant effect on academic performance than intellectual ability.

Turning self-discipline into an organizational habit

Charles Duhigg says in his book The Power of Habit[25] that when you "repeat, repeat, and repeat a routine until you do it naturally, it becomes a *quick-win that* motivates you every day." You have the opportunity to enjoy it; even making your bed can be motivating if you see it as a *quick win.*

He also says that organizations can help employees build these routines. He explains, "what employees need are clear instructions on how to deal with turning points."

---

[25] Charles Duhigg. *The power of habit.* Random House Trade Paperback Edition. 2014.

In their book Analyzing performance problems, Robert Mager and Peter Pipe say[26]: "Keep in mind that if (employees) can do it, but they are not doing it, there is a reason. Only rarely is the reason lack of interest or lack of desire. Most people want to do a good job. When they don't, it's often because of an obstacle in the world around them."

Both agree that what prevents a routine from being maintained is usually an obstacle or a turning point. Therefore, companies need to remove those barriers and train employees to do it themselves.

Let's say you want to get to work and make a specific report first thing in the morning. But, unfortunately, you can't find the information to prepare your report. It gets lost in all that paperwork you have, so you spend 30 minutes organizing it until you find what you need. The result? You send the report late.

"Will power becomes a habit by choosing a certain behavior beforehand and then following that routine when an inflection point arrives.

Charles Duhigg

Use all the knowledge of 5S to help you prepare to be more productive the next day. To not waste time organizing (eliminating the "desk clutter" turning point), you can have a specific compartment to leave everything you need to do your report. When you get to your desk the following day, it should be easy to find everything you need well organized and ready to use, such as a To-Do tray, as in Image 36.

[26] Robert Mager and Peter Pipe. *Analyzing performance problems.*

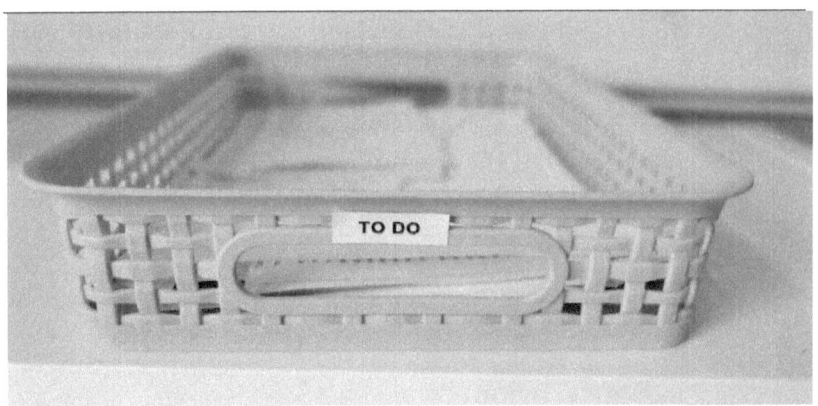

Image 36

If you want to start running, get a treadmill at home, or find a running path close to your house, because if it rains or you don't have the car, you will break the routine. If you want employees to dress appropriately at work, get them a uniform. Facebook CEO Mark Zuckerberg makes it easy to dress up in the morning by always wearing the same thing: Zuckerberg's "work uniform" consists of jeans, sneakers and a gray T-shirt. When asked about his wardrobe in 2014, he told his audience, "I really want to clear my life up so that I have to make as few decisions as possible about anything except how to serve this community best."

Create an environment where doing the right thing is easy. The more people trained in 5S, the easier it is to maintain in the break room, kitchen, logistics, sales, retail, security, administration, HR, manufacturing, warehouse, reception, bathrooms. The 5S committee, mentioned in the chapter HOW TO SUPPORT THE IMPLEMENTATION, should help to align all sectors and remove obstacles.

Self-discipline is part of making every procedure a habit, no matter what it is.

According to a study from Duke University[27], about 45 percent of our daily actions are made up of habits. Our habits, then, are a fundamental reflection of who we are. We become what we frequently do. Success comes from what is repeated, repeated, and repeated until a habit is built, and it is no longer an effort. A soccer player turns pro just by practicing.

To improve self-discipline, you have to practice and repeat new habits. The true habit of self-discipline is meeting standards no matter what, even when no one is looking.

Practice and repeat!
Practice and repeat!
Practice and repeat!

Employees and leaders get frustrated when they think they are not getting results early in the 5S implementation. Regularly viewing before and after photos and audit results are ways to acknowledge continuous improvement.

Leaders are key at this point to support the effort by continually monitoring and highlighting the importance of repeating the habit no matter what. Leaders should take tours and ask questions like the following:

- Why is this tool not in place?
- Why was this list not completed?
- Has this leak been reported?

Leadership, or even peer support, helps employees understand that procedures need to be repeated and repeated until they become part of the daily routine, at least initially. Team routines like meetings are also very important in helping leaders model the correct behaviors. When everyone's meetings are carefully planned and followed, the self-discipline muscle is also strengthened. See more about leading a 5S implementation in the chapter HOW TO PROMOTE IMPLEMENTATION - ROLES.

During the store phase of 2nd S, a board may have been painted with tool shadows (see image 37) to define the "home" for the tools. But what happens when it is not respected and the tools are placed elsewhere?

---

[27] https://dornsife.usc.edu/assets/sites/545/docs/Wendy_Wood_Research_Articles/ Habits/Neal.Wood.Quinn.2006_Habits_a_repeat_performance.pdf

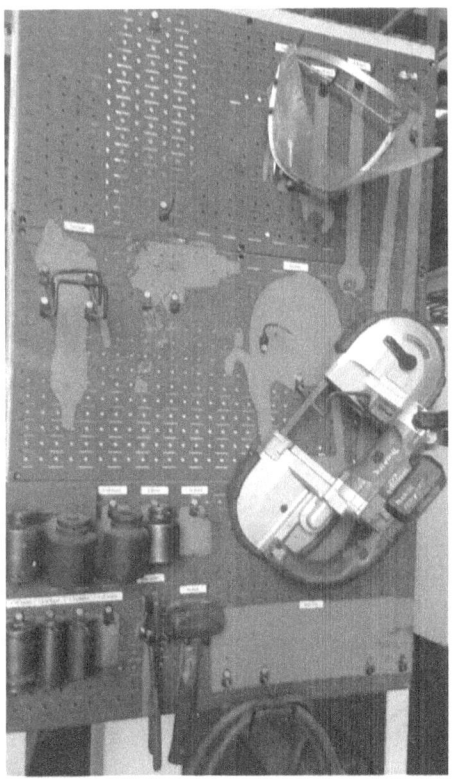

Image 37

This picture shows a typical example of a 5S implementation that is not sustained. The tools have been sorted out (1S - Sort). They have a clearly defined home (2S - Store). There is a rule for cleaning it after use (3S - Shine). There is a routine to have all the tools stored at the end of the shift (4S - Standardize). So...

Why isn't the tool there?

Why is the solder mask not in the right place?

Why isn't the saw positioned correctly?

Typical responses are:

- I had to hurry up for lunch
- I was going to come back soon.
- I had to leave early.
- I was working with it
- The hook for the saw doesn't work well.
- There was a lot of work, and production came first.

After your team has been trained in 5S, you can ask the following questions to help them understand the real cause of the problem.

"You've defined the best place to store your tools; why do you take so long to store them? Remember the rule of the 30 seconds."

"Why are you using so many tools at the same time? Remember to clean them up before using more tools.

"Why are you in a hurry? Shouldn't you always have enough time to put things away and do the work before they cause an accident to someone else? What has caused you any delay?

If the tool hook is not working correctly, have you tried to replace it as part of your continuous improvement efforts?

Shouldn't 5S be part of the production time, not a separate task? Do you need help with the 5S of your process?

So, if a lack of time or lack of proper tools does not allow you to do a good job, then the procedure should be changed to show the actual amount of time needed to do the job. Or the task should be changed so that it can be done with the specified time or tool. Non-compliance is not the answer in 5S. Either it is respected or exposed and fixed, but something can always be done. You are already starting with something by adding the problem to the action plan.

You don't have to adjust everything at once.

Doing things right is contagious

Once the new habits have been internalized through the 15 microsteps, the self-organizing muscle is strong and becomes even stronger with each habit added to the routine. Everyone performs the 5S activities without being forced to do them.

Like termites follow other termites to build the perfect nest, doing the right thing is contagious.

That is why 5S, over time, becomes easier to apply. Like any sport, in the beginning, it is difficult to follow a routine, and after some practice, you become "addicted" to the routine and need to keep practicing.

When teaching 5S and going into the details of, for example, "how to clean a table," it is common for people to get frustrated saying, "it's common sense, why we need to provide specifications and images to show how it should be done." It is because "common sense is the least common of the senses." Therefore, it makes sense not to throw papers out of the trash can; it makes more sense to throw papers in the trash can. Still, we find places where the garbage is outside the trash can. Why? Because everyone else does it, or because it's easier to do it that way. Essentially, we have to make the rules easy to follow and **make "doing the right thing" contagious and easy.**

"Keep looking, don't settle." Steve Jobs

Supporting implementation

Maintain an action plan to follow up on improvement opportunities found in audits and day-to-day activities. Here are some of the things you can do to continue your efforts

- Invite iteration, without fear of failure
- Assigning responsibilities
- Train people
- Organize regular meetings
- Define a 5S day
- Celebrate the team's achievements
- Define a process to update the action plan periodically
- Continue to add ideas to the action plan every week to exercise your self-organizing muscle

Assigning responsibilities

Make sure everyone has a duty to maintain the 5S effort. It's not just for the leaders, the operators, or the maintenance staff. Everyone who uses the facility must be involved in the effort, including new employees, directors, owners, suppliers, contractors, and even customers. Even people who work remotely must be trained and practice 5S at home, too, so that when they visit the facility, they are already prepared.

As long as the standards are clear, everyone can help. It is up to you to make sure that responsibilities are clear and available.

Organize regular meetings

Organize periodic 5S meetings (see HOW TO PROMOTE APPLICATION - Team Routines) To maintain the 5S spirit at the team level. 5S minutes can be done at the beginning or end of any meeting, as well as a safety minute. Everyone can mention a section that needs to work hard on cleaning or an area that did a great job identifying and sectioning. These findings can be shared periodically as *DO's and DONT's.*

You can also arrange daily 5S meetings and 15-minute stand-up meetings at the end or beginning of each shift to discuss action plan updates or urgent improvements to work on. In addition, I recommend at least a monthly meeting with all team members to discuss the audit results and review the action plans to ensure everyone is on the same page and that improvements are continuing.

Train everyone to respect procedures

Companies can help employees see what is within their reach to change and beyond their reach and manage it more efficiently.

Nothing can be controlled 100% of the time. There's always something that can be overlooked. The best control is to train everyone on 5S. Self-organization is about "Doing the right thing even when no one is looking. Involve team members, suppliers, customers, contractors, relatives, neighbors and everyone else by training them in the 5S method. 5S seems counterproductive at times. Team members are not used to focusing on organization or cleanliness. Sometimes it is necessary to unlearn and retrain to learn new habits.

A coach is helpful to accelerate change and to be able to reach more people in less time. Use different methods, from microlearning to practical training in the workplace and individual coaching. Share as much information as possible through articles, videos, photos, podcasts, etc., on how to keep improving. Make it available to all levels of the organization. 5S is easy to understand for both operators and managers. It is easy to learn. Now make it easy to sustain.

Establish a 5S day

5S is an ongoing effort, it is not a one-day event, and you don't want your team to get that idea. Still, 5S days can help launch the initiative or renew motivation.

What can you do on 5S day?

- Give a 5s introductory course
- Meet with the organization's directors and leaders to define the purpose of implementation, standards, objectives and pilot areas.
- Start by dividing the area into sub-sectors with owners
- Start by separating what you don't need. Spend time going through the sectors to highlight what is and what is not required.
- Audit all sections with managers to see differences across areas, best practices and so that employees feel proud of their improvements.
- Celebrate annual achievements in all sectors

Celebrate and acknowledge the team's achievements

Celebration and gratitude should never be overestimated; they are crucial to involve everyone. And they don't always equal an expensive reward. You can thank an individual when you walk by their section and see that something has improved. You can thank employees when you see an update of their action plan. You can thank them at the end of an audit review. You can thank them when they have a question.

Every new habit is a reason to celebrate. It means that the 5S has impacted their lives and the lives of the people around them.

Several companies choose to celebrate with their families. They organize a 5S day with the employees to celebrate the annual achievements and invite their families to visit the facilities and learn and take pictures. After implementing 5S, employees feel proud of their workplace, feel part of it, and see themselves as architects of the organization, cleanliness, quality, safety, and innovation. They want to show their achievements to their families. It is not an event where three employees out of 500 receive an award. It is an event where everyone can feel proud, enriched and rewarded. Intrinsic motivation is much more powerful than extrinsic motivation in making people happy about themselves for more extended periods.

Have a process to update the action plan periodically

Team members, in general, in different industries and cultures, enjoy working the 5S way. They see the results and want to be part of the change. What they usually do not enjoy is reporting improvements.

That's why you'll find it challenging to track improvements other than through audits. Still, it's part of the self-organizing effort to teach them to plan what they want to improve, organize their activities, and be able to carry them out.

The action plan is one of the best ways to track improvements. You can use an Excel spreadsheet. You can use a sheet of paper that teams complete with a simple pen at their workplace. Or the third option is to have an online system that makes it easy for them to add items or ideas. If you don't have your ERP system, you can use my TheWeCulture.com application or download it for free to your phone to get an Action Plan template.

Exercise your self-organizing muscle

That's it. It is the easiest part of the 5S, and the most difficult at the same time. It's easy because all you need to do is practice what you've accomplished so far, but it's the hardest because it's up to you. Exercise your self-control muscle by building these new habits in your life. You decide what is best; you determine what can be eliminated. And always remember that less is more. When you follow the steps of the 5S, always keep in mind that the process is like a ladder: you simply move up small steps, remove the obstacles and keep going up! If you change, the world changes with you. The power is yours to take.

Deliverable microstep #13: Self-organization muscle reinforced through repetition.

14- Observe the current process to remove obstacles

Even when you start small, there will always be obstacles in your way that will make you doubt whether you are doing the right thing or will at least delay you. You have to work first on getting rid of the small barriers that can prevent you from accomplishing it. You need to plan how to deal with those tipping points or situations that will make it more difficult. Now at this point, you must figure out what can go wrong. If your team members are not aligned, they may become a source of friction.

Audits

A familiar way to identify potential barriers to success on your team is to audit the system, checking what might go wrong and how it can be improved. Don't wait until the problem appears (procrastination); be proactive and prevent it. Do not wait until the annual performance evaluation to realize that your team has not worked on 5S. Monitor and provide feedback regularly.

Schedule periodic audits to find barriers and turning points that may delay implementation. Auditing all teams each month helps you see the overall picture of how the implementation is going at the company level. You can compare groups, find common challenges and best practices.

The audit can be internal or external. Many companies choose to do both.

When the audit is internal, it can be done by the team that leads, the manager, or a cross-audit with other teams.

When the audit is external, it is performed by an auditor or a 5S coach. It should not be seen as a threatening moment but as a step towards further learning the method.
Several coaches can take turns evaluating different sections each month and offer a different perspective if there are several coaches. However, if there is only one trainer, the good thing is that they can follow the application of the equipment.

How audits can help prevent errors

There are always many things that can be found in auditing that are not clean, organized or standardized, but the most important thing is to focus on identifying hidden problems such as:

- Gray areas that have no owner
- Areas or employees that are behind with the implementation of 5S or do not respect the values
- Teams or individuals who are impacting other teams. Some employees leave instruments or tools out of place in the area of others. Sometimes the processes are unclear, and team A expects team B to do so, while team B expects the same from team A. The auditor can detect this and facilitate resolution.
- Contractors or new employees who are not 5S trained
- Areas that are only organized for "the visit" are not prepared for a surprise audit. One should be able to audit at any time, as the power of the 5S is that they are organized as you go along, not just for show.
- Offices that do not follow the 5S principles. Whether it is the manager's office or the contractor's rest area, the 5S mentality must be installed everywhere.

Audit report:

The audit report shows the status of each section of the 5S application. It includes a detailed explanation of what the auditor identified as not aligned with the 5S principles or the 5S micro-steps. In addition, it usually includes photos of what can be improved or what has already been improved, a standard checklist by S, a detailed explanation by subsection showing improvements, questions and suggestions about what could be improved based on the 5S standards.

Ideally, audits should be done monthly.

- The checklist helps you see the big picture and different ways to improve and follow the standards of the 5s. At the end of each chapter in this book, there is a 5S audit guide that you can use as a standard *checklist.*
- The detailed comments help to see what could be improved within the subsection in more detail.

Comments should be as specific as possible, such as

"There are hoses and carpets on the floor of section 123. Do you have a home to store them?"

"There is no visible cleaning schedule for the wall xxx"

"There is no updated action plan; the last action item was written two months ago. "

"There's dirt and a leak behind the xyz machine."

"There are samples in the soil. What is the process for storing the samples?"

The comments can also be displayed together with a before and after picture.

The audit comments should then be included in the action plan for each section. Of course, they are only suggestions from the auditor, not an obligation. The auditor should discuss the findings during the audit so that questions can be asked to the workers and observations clarified. Then the team defines which tasks it prioritizes for further improvement.

- A meeting at the end of the tour would help to agree with section members on the next steps.

Experienced teams can also evaluate each other. You do not need to be a process expert to audit; you only need to be a 5S expert. Groups that have already practiced the 4S have the experience of helping and sharing their knowledge with others.

- A rating scale. To evaluate the different sections, you can use the following scale:

Just starting	Basic knowledge	Cons cious Incompetence	Co nscious Competence	U nconscious Competence
0 to 29	30 to 49	50 to 69	70 to 89	90 to 100

You can also apply different weights to each S. Standardizing, and self-organizing are more complicated than the first 3S. You can use 30% weight to the 5th S, 25% weight to the 4th S, and 15% to sort, store, and shine.

The results of the audit:

The comments describe findings such as a procedure not followed, a broken tool not segregated, a leak not reported, a homeless item, or an untrained employee. When an item does not follow the three principles of the 5S, the four values or the five steps, it is a finding. Some of them are quick fixes, like an out-of-place tool.

Others require a deeper understanding of the 5S culture. An example is ensuring that all employees have easy and visual access to team metrics to follow the CARE value of Attention to Detail and Metrics. This value is important for achieving self-organization but may not be crucial for keeping the workplace organized in the short term, so it is neglected. However, knowing the metrics makes team members more accountable for results over time.

This is part of an organization-wide management decision. Therefore, it is worth sharing some complex audit findings at Committee meetings to agree on a joint approach across the company.

> **Tips**
> When auditing, you understand WHY something may go wrong, not WHO is to blame. There is a big difference. Guilt creates resentment and a lack of commitment. The value of CARE helps to increase engagement. It means that you are there to help them, not to lead them, and you rely on the experience and knowledge of your team members.

Define 5S metrics (outstanding tasks, audit score, % of action plan completed, space available, productivity, money spent, time saved)

If you can't measure it, you can't improve it - Peter Drucker

Some consultants start the score from zero each time they do the audit in terms of scores. That is, this month they can get a 70 and next month they can get a 50.

I believe that the scores must be progressive, accumulating the results over time. Seeing an improvement helps the employee to become motivated over time. Some months improve a lot, others are stagnant or only improve a little, and sometimes they go through a crisis and stop doing some things. And many times, it doesn't depend on them but the level of production or team issues. So yes, sometimes they get worse too. I still try not to lower the scores unless the area gets stuck for three consecutive audits, which means a systemic problem doesn't allow them to work in 5s. When a systemic problem is detected, the management or the team should ask for help or provide training tools.

Teams are not stable all the time. Tasks change, people change, and the company changes, so the team and its members must adapt to these changing circumstances. It needs to be taken into account when evaluating 5s, as 5s is part of the job as well.

However, it is essential to always emphasize in the audit what is good and what can be improved, no matter what the circumstances.

At the end of the day, 5S is not more work; it's better work. And the goal of the 5S audit is to help remove barriers and turning points, not just find them.

If you're going to have scores, then you can define metrics. It is not necessary to set a monthly goal, but you can set the desired goal for the end of the year to be in the range of 70-89 Conscious Competition, for example.

As 5S should be seen as an aid to work, not a burden, setting a monthly target can be taken as a burden. You may think that employees need to be pushed to excel, but that shows no respect for them.

5S is about caring for the company, the employee, the customer, the suppliers, the community. To be respectful (CARE - R for Respect) is to think that every employee is doing their best. Essentially, the message is that if you ask for a specific score and the employee cannot achieve it; it is because there is a barrier that prevents them from doing so. If you're going to ask for specific goals every month, then you have to sit down with them every month to see why it was achieved or not. You'll be surprised to see that employees appreciate the support much more than the criticism.

Team evaluation

I suggest that the evaluation is by teams, based on a specific shift or section, between 6 and 10 members. As Jeff Bezos suggests, use the two-pizza rule: if you have a meeting with your 5S team, you should be able to feed them two pizzas, which means you should ideally have 6-8 members, maximum 10. A six-member team is ideal for walking around the different spaces and doing practical exercises.

Individual scores and individual awards are not recommended to avoid silo thinking. They do not help to work as a team; people start thinking in terms of "what's in it for me" and not for us. As discussed in the introduction, 5S should help work as a team and think in terms of "us" not "me." The rewards will be discussed later in the chapter CULTURAL CHANGE.

The other problem with goals and rewards, both individual and team, is that people are so focused on them that people will stop working to achieve them if they are eliminated. The focus on the reward, or the goal itself, takes attention away from the real goal. When people think about becoming a self-organizing team rather than achieving a random goal, the focus becomes clear and satisfactory to all parties.

Avoid any arbitrary monthly targets. Instead, let your team get organized to see what works and what doesn't. They should be able to say what needs to be done. Over time, you can ask them to set their own goals.

Some metrics you can use besides the audit score:
- Number of suggested action items or improvements per section
- Number of audit results
- Number of improvements mentioned in the audit
- Inventory rotation
- Inventory costs
- Number of security incidents
- Number of safety observations to prevent incidents
- Productivity
- Number of hours lost due to unexpected circumstances

These figures can help determine which areas contribute most to the 5S effort, which ones have more problems, and where other departments, such as maintenance or procurement, should be involved. KPIs need to help you discover what is happening and how to solve it, eliminate the root cause, or contain it, and move forward.

Set goals that change over time

As you will see in the last microstep, 5s is a daily effort that never stops. You can never say, "I've finished 5S; what's next?" You never finish; there's always something you can do better. 5s becomes part of your job, so you never leave it behind. If you want to set goals, they have to change over time. You can ask for 80% compliance with the first 3S in the first year. Then in the second year, you can focus on standardization and discipline. Then the following years, it's all about maintaining habits and looking deeper to see more opportunities for improvement.

Typically, personnel, processes and products change over time, so that means you have to adapt your 5S standards continuously.

Maybe the first year, the team will advance 80%, but the following year, they will only improve 10%, which is normal; improvements will be smaller. After some time, every 1% improvement is a challenge and a bigger change.

So you can understand how this works; 5S is like a marathon. You run the first marathon in four hours, and the following year you can run it 30 minutes faster. The following year, you're not likely to run it another 30 minutes faster; maybe you can improve just 10 minutes. The next year you might only get 1 or 2 minutes better. And so on, as long as you keep practicing. When you master a skill, you can keep improving it, but you don't rate your improvements the same way. Maybe improving 2 minutes now is as good as improving 30 minutes the first time.

After a few years in 5s, the improvements are not as evident, but they are still profound, so keep working. You don't need to "finish 5S" to start any other project. 5s has to become part of your way of working. It just helps you to practice your self-control muscle. So don't let it fall off your radar after the second year of trying so hard to get it started.

Deliverable microstep #14: Achieved a seamless process

15- Make micro-changes continuously to improve

Finally, you got to the last microstep of your 5S journey. And although it is the last one, it implies the beginning of a new way of working, where you never stop improving.

A study by the University of Scranton found that **92 percent**[28] of people fail to meet their New Year's resolutions. So, what differentiates a person who can keep their resolutions from one who can't? In her article for Thrive Global, Arianna Huffington proposes starting new habits with a small change or a microstep[29]. "These are small, actionable, science-backed steps you can take to make immediate changes in your daily life. "

And the reasons why reducing new habits to small units work are two. The first is that seeing a very large or long-term goal scares us; it scares us that we won't achieve it. As Arianna says, "The idea is that if we take steps small enough, they will become too small to fail." You have to break down changes and tasks so that they seem achievable, and you don't have to be afraid to start them.

The second has to do with making it so small that it prevents us from multi-tasking. If we have a task to accomplish, like writing a book, for example, which may take several days, months, or even years, it is expected that we will do many other tasks in between. It is called multi-tasking, and it dramatically reduces our productivity when we go from one task to another without finishing any of them. If we at least make sure that the first task is completed before moving on to the next, we would not be multi-tasking.

So, make the habits as small as they allow you not to do another task in between. For some people, it can be an hour. For others, 3 hours. Each one has to define their limit. A book, for example, can be divided into small chapters that you can close before, for example, checking emails or going out to lunch. That way, you'll be sure to finish at least one small piece.

---

[28] https://www.inc.com/marcel-schwantes/science-says-92-percent-of-people-dont-achieve-goals-heres-how-the-other-8-perce.html

[29]https://thriveglobal.com/stories/microsteps-big-idea-too-small-to-fail-healthy-habits-willpower/

Micro-steps are like small batches in a production system, milestones in a project or sprints in the Scrum method. The sprint is not reviewed, and new tasks are not added until the sprint is completed. You don't eat all your 2000 calories in one meal; you divide them up at breakfast, lunch and dinner, right? It's the same mechanism.

For example, if you want to start running, run at least 5 minutes every day. One day it won't hurt. Then you can increase your practice to 10 minutes. And so on. I, for example, enjoy exercising in 10 to 15-minute increments. I've never been as consistent as when I started dividing it up. I want to commit to 30 minutes a day in total, but it can be challenging to achieve. So, I swim 15 minutes at noon; then, I do 15 more minutes of abdominal exercise in the afternoon. It makes it easier to think about stopping 15 minutes for exercising than 30 or an hour. That way, you don't miss the routine.

For example, in the scrum method, it is normal to classify tasks into numbers 1, 2, 3, 5, 8 (The Fibonacci sequence) according to the estimated duration in hours. All assignments should be completed in 1, 2, 3, 5 or 8 hours. Make it as small as you need.

Summarizing, first plan what you want to do, and second, divide it into small habits, which you will add one by one, little by little. 5S was presented in 15 microsteps so that you can learn at least one small habit per week. In 4 months, you should have your 5S sector ready.

What are the new habits that employees learn with 5s?

Some of the new habits
- ✓ Cleaning is part of our daily tasks
- ✓ If it gets dirty, you clean it up right away.
- ✓ Everything you use, you keep when you finish the job.
- ✓ It is vital to keep the signage and procedures up to date
- ✓ If a rule no longer applies, it must be challenged or reported
- ✓ It is necessary to comply with the rules even when no one is looking
- ✓ Report a problem as soon as we detect it

A small improvement is still an improvement.

Start with a pilot team

In the next chapter on implementation and cultural change, you will read that starting with a pilot sector is recommended. As you can see, it is a question of starting with something small.

When one team is taking a class, they improve cleanliness and efficiency. The other teams know about it and will want to do it too.

The pilot team will feel unique for being among the first to implement. However, if you start with all the teams simultaneously, the "unique effect" is lost.

Sections that have not implemented 5s will be evident within a company and will feel embarrassed compared to the rest.

Change is more effective when teams feel the need to be trained (they ask for it, but they are not forced to). They will feel embarrassed and want to show that they can improve too. Healthy competition will begin to push everyone to get the best out of themselves. It is the power of visual management; **everyone can notice the changes.**

Start practicing the new habits one at a time. By making at least one improvement per week, you will have four a month and 48 a year!

Deliverable microstep #15: Processes improved every week, by everyone, everywhere

---

I commit to making one micro change per week.

Implementation Step 5: SELF-ORGANIZATION

- ✓ Daily 5 minute meetings
- ✓ Organizing the committee meetings
- ✓ Use checklists as an audit
- ✓ Cross-sector audit
- ✓ Organize internal and external audits
- ✓ Lead by example: motivating, celebrating, walking the plant, recognizing achievements
- ✓ Communicate in all possible formats
- ✓ Reward expected behavior
- ✓ Show before and after photos
- ✓ Train customers and suppliers in 5s

5S Audit Guide

1) The methodology has been implemented everywhere in the area
2) The team members know the methodology and have the 5S mindset
3) 5S best practices are awarded or recognized by management
4) There is a system to monitor the implementation (e.g., audit, KPI's)
5) There is an action plan to follow up on 5S pending items.
6) Employees are proactively looking for continuous improvement and they document it.
7) Procedures are respected, if not, errors are detected immediately, resolved and prevented in the future.
8) The 5S tasks are unconscious (e.g., you use it, you store it).
9) 5S is applied together with other systems like TPM, ISO 9001, OSHA.
10) Teams meet periodically to discuss 5S status and implementation.

How to practice self-organization in your day-to-day life?

When team members learn the power of self-organization, they want to implement it at home. They will want to use it to organize their room, home office, and kitchen. And especially, they will want to use it to help manage the family. The family should be a clear example of self-organization, with no leader. Everyone knows what needs to be done. Each member has a duty. Every time a member uses a cup, they automatically wash it or put it in the dishwasher. Even the children can organize their room or propose changes.

Implementing 5S at home helps us to communicate and avoid misunderstandings. As mentioned at the beginning of the book, people spend a lot of time looking for things they lose, blaming others for the loss, or getting stressed out.

Let's see how the values of 5S CARE also apply at home. First, 5s helps to ensure that everyone is aware of the tasks needed to maintain the house (CARE - C for connection). When someone in the house is not following the procedures, it is obvious if everything else is working well (CARE - Attention to detail). Third, it reduces community friction and increases mutual respect (CARE - R for respect) for all organization members, regardless of age or experience. Finally, 5S allows everyone to do their part (CARE - E for Empowerment).

Practicing self-organization is all about you. You change; the world changes. Commit to improving a small habit in your daily routine. Don't think about results or scores all the time; think about the purpose and process for achieving them. The results will be seen in the long run.

"When we change, the world changes."

Daisaku Ikeda

5S your mind

Let's now review how to integrate the 5S mentality:

1. Sort: separate what you need to do now from what you can do later to avoid multi-tasking
2. Store: focus on what you have to do now
3. Shine: once you finish a task, leave everything organized and clean before starting the next one.
4. Standardize: define a routine to build new habits
5. Self-organize: repeat the best habits every day and create new ones

Build the 5S habit wherever you are. 5S routines have the spirit of installing a ceremony at the beginning and end of your day. Making the bed every morning as part of a routine is a small accomplishment that you commit to every day and leads, believe it or not, to more meaningful and satisfying results during the day because it puts you in a positive "I can" mode. What you do each day sets the stage for what you will achieve in the long run.

Remember, self-organization is a muscle, and it gets tired at the end of the day, which is when you are usually with your family or friends. If everyone is practicing their respective muscles, they will all work better together at any given time.

If you got this book for some reason, take it as an opportunity to start new habits at home and at work to help you keep your spaces under control. Develop your new 5S routine, and enjoy it every day.

Do you follow all the defined procedures, but feel that not everyone is involved? Implementations of 5S are challenging to sustain unless everyone changes their behavior. It is time to change the culture of the team. Continue with Part II, "5S for leaders".

Download the We Culture app for more free resources and training courses

www.theweculture.com

PART II: 5S for leaders

HOW TO SUPPORT THE IMPLEMENTATION

5S starts at the top, and is sustained at the bottom.

The key to sustaining 5S is actually to work in teams, top and bottom, together. Everyone must work as a system, respectfully with everyone else, ask questions, share information, and empower every role.

In this section, you will learn about the 5S roles, recommended routines and other complementary tools that can help you implement.

Roles

Roles are specific functions that I recommend creating to facilitate the implementation of 5S company-wide. These include:

The 5S Committee

Representatives from all the sections in the organization form the 5S committee. Even if not all the groups are implementing 5S, it would be great to have them all in the meeting.

The 5S committee provides top-down guidance and receives bottom-up input, information, and suggestions on improving the 5S implementation. Communication goes both ways through different communication artifacts. Team members should be welcome to attend the 5S committee meeting to share their success stories, understand the big picture, or simply to cover for an absent representative in order not to lose their vote in any session.

5S committee meetings can be scheduled weekly, bi-weekly or monthly. Face-to-face or remotely. The most important part is to keep a routine to do the meeting periodically and send the agenda in advance to make sure everyone is aware of how they can contribute to the meeting. The agenda can include the following items:

- Attendance checklist: a record of attendance to the meeting
- 5S quick wins: invite everyone, including the trainers, to talk about any updates or best practices that they want to share
- Status of the Management Action plan: just like the teams have an action plan. The management team can have an action plan for global issues. They can track items done, in progress and to be done. Such as:
    - Communication company-wide (newsletters, videos, best practices)
    - 5S implementation in common areas, such as corridors, restrooms or meeting rooms
    - Status on red tags approval and removal
- Audit results and other KPI's
- Training needs
- Next steps

The Leadership role

Many self-organizing teams don't have leaders but facilitators. Instead of using a command and control approach, they coach and help the teams practice the right behaviors. 5S teams can become self-organized for housekeeping and keep the leader for operational work. It's a start.

When organizations have leaders, especially if they have several layers of leadership, the leadership role in a 5S implementation is critical to avoid pitfalls.

In these organizations, leadership support is vital, as in every other type of company-wide implementation. Leaders teach by example, provide resources, provide guidance, assign priorities and facilitate the distribution of assignments. Culture is an imitation game.

As 5S is intrinsically a way to help team members self-organize, leaders may feel confused. Some may overtake some of the tasks, micromanaging and doing it all to show improvement through time. Others may remain totally out of the loop as if 5S was not part of their job description.

The leader's role in 5S is to facilitate the implementation. The main tasks are:

- Assigning owners to every section, ensuring there are no gray areas
- Reviewing action plans to make sure everybody is onboard

- Helping employees assign priorities to the different tasks and resources needed
- Looking for help from other departments such as maintenance, procurement, quality or HR
- Reviewing the audits with the auditor and sharing them with the employees
- Establishing team routines such as meetings, "thank you" events or training sessions
- Helping to define standards
- Sharing best practices across other teams

For every step of the 5S, there are specific activities that the leaders can work on to facilitate the implementation. Below is a table showing these actions also aligned to the CARE habits.

	CONNECTION	ATTENTION	RESPECT	EMPOWERMENT
1S	Develop a red tag process plant-wide	Review action plans periodically	Respect employee's decision to remove items and offer support	Assign ownership
2S	Make sure there are no grey areas by sharing your concerns with other departments	Provide resources	Thank employees in front of others, and share success pictures	Facilitate prioritization of tasks and distribution common spaces
3S	Organize cleaning efforts in common areas	Ask why, do not provide solutions or quickly um to conclusions	Set the example to clean after yourself when a meeting is over or work is done	Review the section map of dirty places periodically and provide support

4S	Define team routines like audits, team audit reviews, committee meetings and standup meetings	Share team metrics, 5S steps, company purpose and objectives in common areas, TVs, banners, flyers and whiteboards	Be the first to respect standards set by others	Make sure cleaning schedules are available and recognized by all personnel
5S	Look for common issues across other sections and find shared solutions	Share team audit results at the workshop, do walkarounds asking questions and schedule personal audits	Practice self-control to get along with others	Continue training and empowering personnel

1)   Start by removing what you don't need. Develop a red tag process plant-wide so that everyone understands how to handle the sorting phase. If this process is not transparent, employees will not be willing to throw away or remove items from their workplaces due to fear or confusion, "just in case."

The red tag process should include the procurement of tags, instructions on how to fill in the tags, and a dollar threshold for items in the ledger. Some companies choose to segregate the items within their section. Some companies choose to have a common area for red tags.

Then there should be a process to decide what needs to stay or be removed, donated, or moved to another section. The committee meeting can determine what to do with these items, or the team members can visit the red tag areas and decide if they need any of the tagged items.

2)   Review action plans periodically; they should be available at the workstation. Associates can post them close to their workstation, on a

shared whiteboard, or they can be stored online in The We Culture App. These action plans must be available for other managers and team members to see them. If the owner leaves the area, the action plan remains in the same place, just like a standard document.

3)   Respect the employee's decision to remove items and offer support. If you, as a leader, recommend not to throw away or remove any of the employee suggestions, the employee will feel frustrated and will no longer sort. So if you disagree, probably the main reasons are two: either the employee is new and needs to learn the sorting and red tag rules (which if there are none should be created), or you are merely procrastinating to make the decision. I have seen piles of items stored just in case because nobody decides what to do with them. In the meantime, these items represent money lost in insurance, space rental, cleaning and potential risks. Coach the employee to make better decisions or review the elements together to make a sound decision, but don't just delay the burden.

4)   Sort action items by owner, and help the employee follow-up on the tasks outside their scope. Report action items in the 5S committee meeting when needed. It is useful to report them when they are out of the team's reach or impact other organizations. One of the roles of the committee is to remove impediments.

5)   Ensure there are no grey areas, meaning areas with no owner or the owner is not clear. Having two owners is as bad as no owners. Share your concerns with other departments to ensure all the areas are taken care of.

6)   Ask what the employees need, especially during coaching sessions, and provide the employee with resources such as dividers, drawers, labels or tools.

7)   Thank employees in front of others, showcase success pictures and appreciate hard work.

8)   Facilitate prioritizing action items and distribution of common spaces to help the 5S implementation move along and reduce the major obstacles through time.

9)   Organize cleaning efforts in common areas, such as share drawers, security offices, storage rooms, meeting rooms, restrooms, waiting rooms, break rooms etc.

10)   Do not provide solutions; ask why to the section owner. They probably know how to solve the issue, but they may not be used to sharing their ideas. Help them speak up by asking how they would solve the problem, who could help them and how it could be prevented or contained.

11)   Set the example to clean after yourself when a meeting is over or work is done.

12)   Review the section map of dirty places periodically and provide support: help the employee analyze the sources of dust, dirt and spills to avoid near misses and accidents.

13)   Ensure all the processes are standardized and define team routines like audits, team audit reviews, committee meetings and standup meetings.

14)   Share team metrics, 5S steps, company purpose and objectives in common areas, TVs, banners, flyers and whiteboards. Organize meetings with other groups or report cleaning issues in a 5S committee meeting when needed

15)   Be the first to respect standards set by others. Remember that keeping clean is everybody's task all the time. Support and guide procedure development for each position, remember common sense is the least common of all the senses.

16)   Make sure cleaning schedules are available and respected by all personnel. Provide time and training for the employees to apply the procedures.

17)   Look for common issues across other sections. Find solutions and best practices working together in cross-functional teams.

18)   Share team audit results at the workshop, do your own walkaround asking questions, and periodically schedule short audits (just a product or a process line). You will keep your team engaged if you start asking about new developments, action plans and challenges.

19)   Practice self-control to get along with others and improve your self-organization skills.

20)   Continue training and empowering personnel, including contractors, janitors, co-ops, office personnel, security, and especially new employees and team leaders. Training is never enough. Use one-on-one sessions to mentor your team members regularly, especially when specific sections are behind or certain behaviors are not sticking in their routines.

First steps:
✓ Apply what you have learned in your section
✓ Keep the action plan updated at all times. You can check each of them in your periodic walkarounds or team meetings. Be prepared for external audits, tell the auditor the improvements done, and the issues to work on. Always keep an open mindset to listen to recommendations and suggestions.

✓ Ask for support from other teams or departments in the committee meetings to make 5S a company-wide effort.

The 5S Coach

Cultural change is not easy. It requires behavior changes ingrained in the way the company operates, starting from the leadership team. That is why a coach comes in handy to facilitate the transition and help people see things differently.

Some companies decide to start the 5S implementation by themselves, which is fantastic from the self-organization point of view, but not ideal unless the internal coach is:

- an expert in the 5S culture
- not embedded with the company culture

Some companies hire coaches only to deliver the introductory training and expect it to be enough to change the culture. However, associates usually need continued hands-on support for some time to change habits and behaviors.

"We cannot solve our problems with the same thinking we used when we created them."

Albert Einstein

Coaches help train people to see with a different lens.

Some companies decide to start with an external coach and continue with internal coaches in the long term. This approach can be effective if the internal coach can help sustain the 5S routines and the management supports them. However, if management doesn't support the implementation, it is little what an internal or external coach can do to sustain the effort.

The 5S coach assists the organization in several ways, including:

- providing 5S training to associates, leaders, suppliers, customers, new hires etc.
- supporting during the on-site implementation
- facilitating the development of standards, schedules and processes like the red tag process
- facilitating meetings
- suggesting communication media

- recommending coaching sessions for specific teams, leaders or individuals
- coaching team members during the implementation
- performing audits
- mediating or communicating cross-functional issues if required
- identifying gray areas, laggard teams and training needs

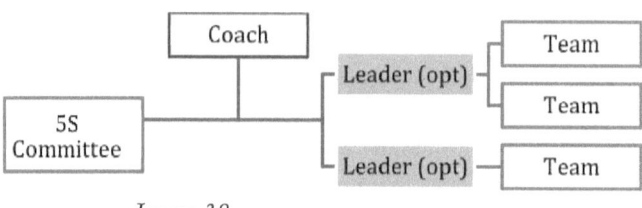

Image 38

Team routines

Now that you know the steps and microsteps, you can use specific routines to make your 5S implementation easier when working in teams.

Team routines are repetitive team activities recommended to plan and coordinate across teams during the 5S implementation to ensure standardization and self-organization at the same time.

Committee meeting

This meeting can be weekly, bi-weekly or monthly, depending on the pace of the implementation, and it is recommended for teams with leaders or self-organized teams.

The objective of the meeting is to share best practices, concerns, goals, audit results and resolve common issues.

Some common issues that may surface are grey areas (areas with no apparent owners), plant-wide standards, red tag process, communication within the organization.

Audit

The audit is an on-site inspection of the different sections applying the 5S culture. The coach usually executes the audit to monitor the progress of the implementation on a monthly or bi-monthly basis. The audit is not just an inspection but a coaching time. The coach walks around the areas with the leader or the team members to see improvements and identify action items to continue improving. The coach can take pictures if the company allows preparing before-after signs. It is recommended to audit all the sections, even if not all the employees have been trained yet. It's the first approach to coaching them on where to start the implementation and how until they all get trained.

Team meeting

The team meeting is an instance of sharing 5S action items, ideas, and suggestions and prioritizing them with team members and leaders. It can be face-to-face or also remote to include anyone involved. The team meeting is also useful for root cause analysis of a complex issue. The team meeting can be a standalone meeting, just a 5-minutes session as part of an operational team meeting or a 15-minute stand-up meeting to share updates and action items when the shift changes.

Audit team review

Team meeting to review the audit results, assign owners to the findings and prioritize action plans. The objective f the meeting is not to solve all the issues but to get better for the next audit.

Walkarounds Training sessions

The walkarounds are sessions where the coach walks around the sub-section with the team members to identify together items to work on. These sessions help the team members see with a different lens their workplaces, not as a worker but as external observers.

Tools to complement 5S

Throughout the book, you have read about various quality tools that are commonly used with 5S. Now it's time to introduce them more in detail. The appendix doesn't include a comprehensive list but includes all the tools that I have used in all the 5S implementations I observed.

The Five why's

To identify the root cause of a problem, Toyota's Taiichi Ohno urged workers to ask "Why" five times.

The 5 Why's is a root cause analysis technique used to identify the root cause of a problem. It is often used to analyze a real error that has occurred.

By asking, "Why?" five times, you should be able to understand a problem deeply enough to identify the ultimate root cause.

Enlist knowledgeable team members to ensure critical X's are identified and understood.

How to implement it with 5S:
Use it to find the root cause of dirt, leaks and disorganization.

Steps to develop 5 Why's analysis
1) Describe the problem as a question.
2) Ask "why" - what are the first level *causes* of the problem?
3) Write each cause on the template
4) For each cause, ask "Why" again and enter answers in the next column
5) Keep asking "Why" until no more answers can be suggested. By the time you have asked "Why" five times, you are usually at the root cause
6) Use the final causes suggested to generate possible solutions
7) Use data to accept/reject each proposed cause
8) Apply the proposed solution
9) Verify that it solved the problem. If the problem is solved, standardize it for other areas. If it was not solved, continue asking why.

Example:
Problem Statement - The car will not start

Why - The battery is dead

Why - The alternator is not functioning

Why - The alternator belt has broken

Why - The alternator belt was well beyond its useful service life and has never been replaced

Why - The car has not been maintained according to the recommended service schedule

Fishbone diagram

The 5why's can also be used as part of the Fishbone diagram analysis, also known as Ishikawa or Cause and Effect Diagram. The Fishbone Diagram is a brainstorming tool designed to identify possible causes of a problem. You should enlist knowledgeable team members to ensure the critical problems and potential causes are identified and understood.

By asking why on each cause, you get to analyze several branches or "spines" of the fish. You can define the categories you want to use, do an affinity diagram to group the causes or simply choose categories from the standards below to help you brainstorm and organize the solutions.

How to implement it with 5S:

Use it to find and analyze various root causes of dirt, leaks and disorganization.

Developing a Problem Statement
- Identify error (e.g. lateness, inconsistency, inaccuracy)
- Identify object (process output) under study

Commonly used categories:
The 6M:
- Machinery/equipment
- Methods/procedures
- Materials (incl. information)
- Manpower (Workforce)
- Medium or Environment (physical as well as the human aspect)
- Measurement

Or
- Failure reasons by process step

Or
- Defect breakdown by component

For example, why are there delays in an operating room? The main causes may be: personnel, materials, equipment, methods used. Bones can then be added to the leading cause: Why do staff cause delays? Because of a lack of training, because of a lack of communication. Step 3: Why is there a lack of training? Because a new operating room was opened and new employees were hired who were not trained.

You can define the categories you want to use for the primary spines. You can first make an affinity chart or simply choose categories from the commonly used ones above to help you brainstorm and organize solutions.

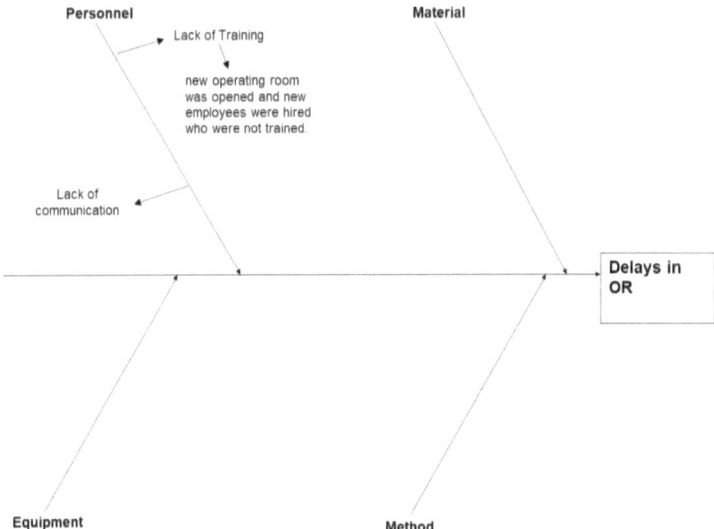

This method helps to organize the information by category, explore different points of view, and analyze unexplored causes that may have been overlooked.

Steps to develop a Fishbone Diagram
1. Locate a room with plenty of wall space
2. Place a flip chart with white paper and draw a fishbone
3. Get agreement on the problem statement and write it on the head: Indicate desired direction such as decrease, increase, lower,

raise; Identify defect (e.g., lateness, inconsistency, inaccuracy) or Identify object under study.

4. Have the group take 2 minutes to write down their own ideas as to the cause of the problem being studied
5. Ask the person submitting an idea to identify in which category to place it. You can use the suggested commonly used categories to help team members think out of the box
6. Place the idea on the spines
7. Build on ideas - repeatedly ask, "Why might this happen?" and add smaller spines to the fish
8. Your team can use "multi-vote" to narrow down the list
   - each team member get three colored sticky dots, that is, three votes
   - silently place the three dots on your top choices (you can put several on the same option to highlight its importance)
   - Pick the top four or five to investigate based on vote counting
   - Test for reasonableness

Best practices

- When doing the brainstorming to build on ideas, don't prejudge and don't allow one person to dominate the session: all opinions are good ideas at this point.
- Treat the fishbone chart as a living document - add ideas to it in the normal course of work
- Use post-it notes to capture ideas, but transcribe these electronically
- Ask why five times or more – get down to a cause with a preventive or mitigating control that can be applied.
- When the brainstorm is over, the real work begins - proving the relationship between cause and effect
- Not all ideas on the fishbone will be of equal importance - prioritize to focus additional data collection (multi-voting works well for this)

FMEA - Failure Mode and Effect Analysis

You can also identify potential problems before they even occur. FMEA or Failure Mode and Effect Analysis is a systematic approach used to identify potential issues ("failure modes") and quantify the risk of occurrence. It is recognized as one of the eight most commonly used tools in Six Sigma projects.

It drives a detailed understanding of what is being studied, produces a risk profile of all predicted failures, and enables follow-up actions to be prioritized based on pre-defined criteria.

The FMEA started to be used in the 1950s, was implemented during the Space Program in the 1960s, and spread to various other industries but predominant in automotive, aeronautics, defense and electronics.

The main elements are:

Failure Mode: A statement that describes how a product or process could fail to meet the intended function or process requirement. Failure modes are observed or have an external effect (noticed by the customer).

Cause: An explanation of how the failure mode could occur. Causes should be described in terms of something that can be corrected or controlled

Example: I (Missed the Meeting) EFFECT because the (Alarm Clock didn't go off) FAILURE MODE

How to implement it with 5S:

Use it to help you standardize processes, improve maintenance and determine failure modes in advance.

What FMEA Addresses

- The intended function of the product/process
- Possible performance failures
- Effects of the failure
- The severity of the effect on the customer
- Possible causes of the failure
- What is being done to detect or prevent the cause
- How effective is the detection or prevention

- What corrective actions can be taken to improve the prevention or detection

Benefits:
- Improved customer satisfaction
  - Fewer product failures experienced by a customer
- Cost Avoidance
  - Fewer engineering changes
  - Less rework
  - Less time and money spent troubleshooting
  - Reduced Business Operating Costs
    - Sales and marketing
    - Order processing and Delivery
    - Product Warranty Costs
    - Potential for liability suits

Types of FMEA
1) Design FMEA: To develop or modify products and components
2) Process FMEA: To develop or modify workflow and processes
3) FMEA MSR: To monitor the functioning of systems

Best practices
- Should be performed early in the design cycle
- Should use a team with diverse experience and expertise
- FMEA is a living document that evolves through time
- FMEA's save time in the long run (preventive vs. corrective)
- Management support and team understanding are keys to success
- Proper FMEA planning avoids pitfalls

Steps to develop a FMEA
1) Planning and preparation
   a. Define the intent, team composition, timing, task allocation and the tools.
2) Structure analysis
   a. Review or develop a simplified process flow-chart
   b. List the purpose of process steps
3) Function analysis

    a. Describe functions in detail. If drilling is the function, the correct way to describe it is drilling a hole with a diameter of 5mm.

    b. Analyze what you need the function for and how do you implement the function. The more precise you are describing the failure mode, the easier it is to analyze it.

4) Failure analysis

    a. Identify failure effects, failure modes and failure causes.

    b. List all possible failure modes of each step before moving on to effects. Some examples of what could go wrong with the function are: sudden failure, failure over time, uninterrupted operation, going at higher levels, lower levels or at the same level, unintended function executed or wrong direction taken.

    c. Complete a list of all effects for each failure before moving on to next failure

    d. Consider every stakeholder in the analysis: suppliers, customers, end consumers and government.

5) Risk analysis

    a. List all the means to prevent and detect each failure effect and the different causes for each effect

    b. Use established criteria to estimate the severity of each effect. Input from actual "customers" is most valuable (severity rating)

    c. Brainstorm process changes that could contribute to the listed effects

    d. Estimate the likelihood the stated cause will occur (occurrence rating)

    e. List all controls that currently exist that would prevent the cause from occurring (Occurrence rating)

    f. Estimate the effectiveness of controls that now exist to prevent the stated cause (Detection rating)

    g. Multiply severity x occurrence x detection to get the RPN (The Risk Priority Number). In the automotive industry, the RPN is not used anymore; what is used is the Action Priority, which is high, medium or low.

6) Optimization
    a. Prioritize the issues to work based on the AP High (must define suitable actions), medium (should define suitable actions), or low (can define further actions).
    b. Define Follow-up actions based on the AP linked to the stated cause to be effective
    c. FMEA owner assigns responsibility
    d. FMEA owner follows up with people with assigned responsibilities
    e. Share progress and status reviews

7) Results documentation
    a. List completed actions on the FMEA form
    b. Submit completed FMEA forms to process owner for review and comment

TPM - Total productive maintenance

5S is key to ensuring equipment maintenance. Implementing the 4S Standardize is also very common to build a TPM approach. TPM is Total Productive maintenance, "an innovative approach to maintenance that optimizes equipment effectiveness, eliminates breakdowns, and promotes autonomous operator maintenance through day-to-day activities involving the total workforce." [30] In simple words, shop-floor employees commit to handling and maintaining the equipment.

Total productive maintenance (TPM) is an organization-wide effort to reduce loss due to equipment failure, slowing speed, and defects.

TPM reduces downtime, service/process interruptions, maintenance waste, costs, prolongs the life of facilities, vehicles, and equipment, and improves quality and customer satisfaction.

TPM is typically implemented after 5S because it helps to set the stage for the success of TPM, ensuring tools are kept clean, and failures are visible.

TPM was born when Seiichi Nakajima combined American maintenance practices with total quality control and full employee involvement in the early 1970s.

---

[30] Seiichi Nakajima. *Introduction to total Preventive Maintenance*. Productivity Press. 1988

In many plants, employees maintain or repair their equipment. Some know how to do it, but they are not allowed to because it's a maintenance department job.

TPM promotes more effective maintenance when it is a shared responsibility between maintenance personnel and operators. Operators should be trained for routine inspections, cleaning, maintenance and minor repairing. The objective is to reduce wastes and losses incurred in equipment operation: zero breakdowns and zero defects.

The maintenance department doesn't go away, but maintenance jobs are organized differently. Operators don't learn to do all the maintenance work but understand how to detect issues and communicate them to the maintenance department to improve prioritization and effectiveness. Some companies that already work as self-organized teams don't need a specific maintenance department. Their members are part of multidisciplinary teams that also include operators, engineers, marketing, and quality experts. However, maintenance tasks are so vital that they become part of the production process.

The essential features of TPM are:
1. Activities to maximize equipment effectiveness
2. Autonomous maintenance by operators (self-organization again!)
3. Company-led small group activities.

When starting TPM, the company needs to bear the expenses of restoring the equipment to its proper condition, training operators, and coaching maintenance and operators to work together. As production increases, costs are covered by the profits obtained, just like it works with 5S.

How to implement it with 5S:

Use it to help you improve equipment maintenance, promote collaboration with other departments, and increase self-organization and self-maintenance. TPM promotes autonomous activities but can't be implemented until a favorable environment allows employees to be autonomous. 5S establishes this environment; it is usually implemented before TPM.

Objectives:

- Promote self-organizing teams, autonomy and teamwork across groups
- Achieve the maximum effectiveness of equipment.
- Involve all equipment operators in developing maintenance skills.

- Improve the reliability of the equipment.
- Reorganize maintenance staff
- Avoid unplanned equipment downtime and its associated costs
- Achieve an economic balance between prevention costs and total costs while reducing failure costs

Benefits:
- ✓ Breakdowns reduced
- ✓ Rate of operation increased
- ✓ Claims from clients reduced
- ✓ Defects reduced
- ✓ Reduction in costs: workforce, maintenance costs and energy conserved
- ✓ Stock reduced
- ✓ Zero or fewer accidents
- ✓ Less pollution
- ✓ Increase in improvement ideas submitted
- ✓ Employee morale and engagement improved

Steps to implement TPM
1) Introduce TPM to top Management and discuss the following:
    i. Define boundaries and goals of the maintenance group
    ii. Team and section new roles and responsibilities
    iii. Review current procedures. Do you have maintenance days scheduled? Do you start maintenance based on specific needs?
    iv. Define new maintenance procedures and long term planning
    v. Define preventive maintenance and equipment checklists standards
2) Provide training to management and employees on TPM
    i. Preventive maintenance through 5S activities
        1S: Inventory of tools required, testers and equipment
        2S: Equipment identification
        3S: Equipment housekeeping
        4S: Visual management
        5S: Audits
    ii. Planning efficient shutdowns
    iii. Failure analysis

      iv.   Specific technical training in lubrication, electrical safety, or others as needed to be able to manipulate the equipment.

3) Implementation in pilot teams
      i.   Just like you did with 5S, start TPM activities in a small group, that can promote the best practices to the rest.
      ii.   You can also create a TPM management committee

4) Improve equipment effectiveness of each piece of equipment experiencing a loss, especially the ones suffering from chronic losses

5) Establish an autonomous maintenance program for operators: Identify equipment, type of issues, and preventive maintenance sheets. Maintenance can do this together with the operators. At this point, operators should already know the importance of checking in the box of the maintenance sheet and taking it as an essential responsibility. Operators should have defined in the 3S shine the basic conditions that should apply to their equipment, now they find out the best way to prevent deterioration and keep it "brand-new." Employees will learn to clean, lubricate, bolt and inspect.

      Equipment can be critical and non-critical, start with the most critical, and with chronicle issues.

6) The maintenance team will have to set their own maintenance calendar and standards, coordinated with the autonomous maintenance activities of the operations. There must be a clear division of the responsibilities of each department.

7) Continue training operators to improve maintenance skills

8) Update maintenance schedule with the equipment, to make sure early maintenance is done and employees are trained accordingly

9) Promote continuous improvement- Follow the 15th micro-step and change every week.

Just like 5S, operations and maintenance departments may have more workload, teaching and learning the new practices at the beginning of the implementation. It can be handled through overtime and subcontractors because it should be temporary. Leaders should allow more time for the operators to perform new tasks. In the long term, the maintenance work will be diminished, and the number of breakdowns and critical situations will decrease.

POKA-YOKE

Poka-Yoke means "to avoid (yokeru) inadvertent errors (poka)" in Japanese.

Mistake Proofing or *poka-yoke* is the practice of striving for zero defects using techniques, standards and devices that prevent errors from being made.

It also provides for detection of and stopping mistakes before they become defects by using shutdown, control, or warning methods.

Mistake proofing determines methods that will ensure a process is defect-free all the time. It applies to any process where repetitive steps occur, which could be skipped, performed out of order, or not conducted correctly. Mistake proofing ensures that tasks can only be done the right way.

Examples:
- Automatic shutoff irons
- Ground fault interrupters (GFCI)
- Tamper-proof caps
- Pilot light shut-offs
- Two hand interlocks
- Keyed connectors
- Airbags
- Neutral interlock
- Buzzers

Mistake proofing principles: Always use the highest principle possible

How to implement it with 5S:
Use it to expose defects or potential mistakes.

Common errors
1) Forgetfulness (not being focused, distracted)
2) Errors due to a misunderstanding
3) Errors in identification (view incorrectly, too far away or too small)

4) Mistakes made by untrained workers
5) Willful failures (ignore rules)
6) Inadvertent errors (distraction, fatigue
7) Errors due to delay in decision-making
8) Errors due to lack of standards (written & visual)
9) Surprise errors (machine not capable)
10) Intentional errors (sabotage – least common)

Technique	Prevent	Detect
Shutdown	When an error is about to be made	When an error or defect has been made
Control	Errors are impossible	Defective items can not move to the next step
Warning	Something is about to go wrong	Immediately when something goes wrong

Steps to implement mistake proofing
1) Describe the defect and determine the defect rate.
2) Identify the operation where the defect is *made* and where it is *discovered*.
3) Map the sequence of events in operation.
4) WATCH the operation being done; detail steps that differ from standard.
5) Identify error conditions that might contribute to the defect (ask 5 why's)
6) Identify the Mistake Proofing device and its technique (Stop, Control, Warn).
7) Try out the Mistake Proofing device. If it doesn't work, try again. Operators can help in evaluating worst-case scenarios.

Mistake proofing devices:
- Color coding items in the process to ensure the correct piece is chosen for an assembly operation
- Shaping parts differently to avoid picking or assembly errors
- Notches in sections will also avoid picking or assembly errors
- Auto-detection (i.e., spell checkers) allow mistakes to be caught before delivery

- Checklists are a very simple way to ensure that omissions and errors have an opportunity to be detected before delivery

The images below show how you can color-code a hose or tube to know its content, or you can shade a tool board to make it easy to know when something is missing before you leave your shift.

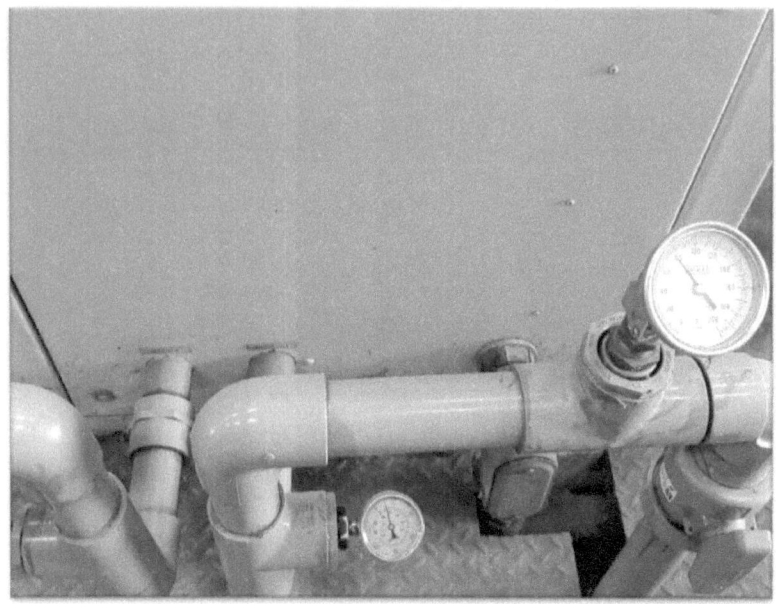

Image 39

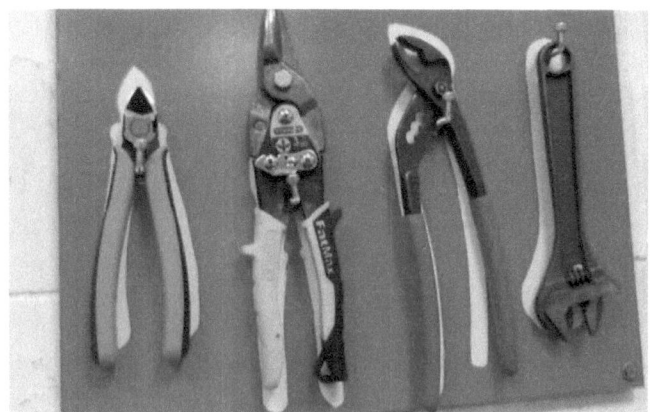

Image 40

Kanban

Kanban is a visual method for controlling production; it is basically a demand scheduling system Toyota developed for efficiency and quality, as part of Just in Time (JIT) and Lean Manufacturing.

As part of a pull system, it uses signals from the customer (next process) to define what needs to be produced. Its purpose is to ensure that you only provide what the customer is asking for and nothing more.

Kanban means "sign." When you see it, you know it is time to manufacture the next part. It eliminates management's daily or weekly schedules to allow for self-organization. Employees know what to produce based on customer information that is communicated from workstation to workstation. The production is not based on estimates or past data but on current information.

Kanbans can take many forms, but the standard ones are Kanban cards or bins to produce or replenish materials.

Operations detail the product, where it is used, and the quantities that should be there. When a process finishes using the materials to which the Kanban card is attached, the card is returned to the previous process.

For replenishment, you can also use bins or colored spaces to alarm when replenishment is needed. Some companies have a red sign outside a drawer to indicate the drawer needs to be refilled. Other companies choose to place empty bins or cards on top of the drawer to show what needs to be replenished. Other simply color in green and red the space dedicated to a specific component so that whenever the red is reached (safety stock), it is a reminder to order more.

You can have 2-bin Kanban systems or 3-bin systems so that whenever you finish a bin, you just retrieve the second one and leave the empty one out to indicate replenishment is needed. It is used a lot in the pharmaceutical and healthcare industry to replenish bins of medicines.

How to implement it with 5S:

Use it to pace the flow of products in a manufacturing process, replenish materials, or organize work using a virtual or physical board.

Benefits:
- Employee engagement because it promotes self-organization

- Less inventory because replenishment is just on time
- No time spent on scheduling production
- No waiting time for production approvals
- Helps to identify bottlenecks
- Less overproduction
- Visible to all stake-holders
- Agile response to changing demands

The system is popular due to its simplicity. It is recommended to be used with 5S to visualize what needs to be done.

Apart from Toyota, another famous company that uses Kanban is the fashion retailer Zara "to renovate stock and move a product from concept to market in weeks.[31]

Kanban thinking is also used as a method used to visualize ways to plot out projects and workflows using columns and cards in Agile implementations. Kanban is similar to the Scrum method, but while Scrum is used to solve complex issues, Kanban is used to solve simple problems or projects. It helps teams see progress and spot blockers. You can create Kanban boards online with tools like Trello or Asana.

This tool is very common in IT and small projects or startups. It's perfect for solopreneurs and business owners because it helps to focus on one thing at a time and expose pending tasks.

Main principles guiding Kanban:

- Visualize work: using whiteboards or virtual boards to organize tasks
- Limit work in progress: limit to one task in progress at a time. If you need to do several tasks, you need to divide them into smaller pieces to do one at a time. It helps you focus and avoid multitasking.
- Measure: it allows you to track progress and ensure there is always something to be done.
- Analyze and improve: it shows a bottleneck or a problem in the workflow.

Steps to implement Kanban board

---

[31] Josh Wright. Kanban: The complete Guide to Managing work as it moves along the process and maximizing the efficiency of the agile and lean project team through the visual methodology on the strategy board. 2020.

All you need to do the Kanban method is a board, physical or digital. The board will be divided into different columns that may vary based on your needs. The columns are usually:

- TO-DO
- DOING
- DONE

You can divide your tasks into sprints or projects, and then after the TO-DO, you add a column for Sprint backlog, where you will include the tasks from the TO-DO that yOu want to accomplish in the sprint.

As an entrepreneur, you can simply divide your work into weeks. So it would work as follows:

- TO-DO: include all the tasks you need to accomplish
- WEEK: add all the tasks that need to be done this week, prioritized, so you put on top the ones that you need to first
- DOING TODAY: only the task that you are doing in the new hour
- DONE: once you finish the task you are doing, you move it to the DONE. At the end of the week, you can monitor how many you accomplished and what is missing.

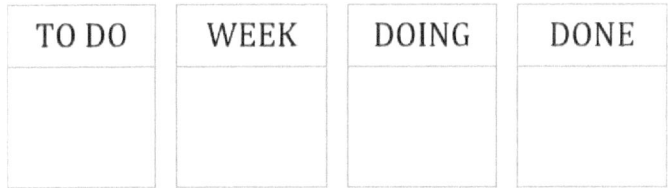

Image 41

Main considerations:

- You only need to do one task at a time
- You can share the board with your team, as long as you make sure everyone does only one task at a time and choose tasks to continue work from the Week or sprint column.

- You only move the task to DONE if it meets some requirements you or the team define. Agile methods promote finishing tasks more than starting them. If you move to done, it means that the work is fully done, reviewed and approved.

- Take the task "reply to an email." There are several steps to accomplish it. If you just wrote it, it doesn't mean it's done. You probably need to review it and then send it o the right person. Until you send it, the task is not accomplished. So DONE means that you do the three steps. Sometimes we underestimate the amount of time required for tasks, assuming it is only "writing the email," while it actually takes longer than that. The secret of time management through Kanban is to estimate the right time for each task and not start another one until that one is truly finished. The time lost when you switch from one task to another is huge. You may take up to 30 minutes to re-focus again on the task at hand after a call, a social media check-in, or a snack time. That's why Kanban helps you to time-box your tasks.

Remember that to incorporate new habits, it's better to start small. If you want to start a big project, divide it into smaller pieces, time-box them in lots of 1 to 3 hours and post them in your Kanban board.

SMED

SMED is a series of techniques pioneered by Shigeo Shingo to **reduce the time it takes to** complete equipment changeovers. SMED means Single Minute Exchange of Die.

Shigeo Shingo started to reduce Japanese manufacturing equipment downtime. The changeover is the process of converting a line or machine from running one product to another. It is just as relevant in the front office or operating room. Experience shows that change can be dramatically reduced by as much as 94% over time. Formula 1 cars use it to improve tires' changeover time.

Watch this youtube video as an example:
https://www.youtube.com/watch?v=UlIGI3laGAo

It was made famous by Toyota's 1000 ton press.

- Traditionally it took two weeks.
- In 1969 the design changed to 4 hrs
- It was first reduced from 4 hours to 90 mins
- Six months later it was reduced 90 mins to 3 mins

"The most dangerous kind of waste is the one we don't recognize" Shigeo Shingo

---

One of my favorite examples is an airline. Southwest, the most profitable airline today, can "changeover" an airplane between flights in less than 30 minutes. Airlines make money when their planes are in the air. They do not make money waiting at a gate.

Why would you need quick changeovers:

1) Maximize production
2) Minimize your customer's interruption
3) Maximize flow to focus on the task at hand
4) Reduce downtime costs

The aim is to reduce the time it takes to switch from the last "good" part of product A to the next "good" part of product B. It is similar to what was reviewed with the Kanban method, the problem is not in the task itself, but the time spent switching from one task to another. For example, if one task takes only one hour, and you spend 30 minutes changing it, that reduces your productivity by 50%.

How to implement it with 5S:

Use it to determine what is needed and what is not. You can define a home for the changeover materials, to help you identify which materials are required during internal or external tasks. Used with visual management, it helps to determine what needs to be ready before the process starts.

SMED benefits

✓ Reduces preparation and unproductive time

✓ Reduces stock and batch size

✓ Increases type of models produced in a certain period

✓ Increases customer satisfaction (e.g., lead time)

✓ Reduces inventory costs and risks

✓ Improves safety at work

✓ Reduces people effort

✓ Increases motivation

✓ Simplifies changeover

Steps to implement SMED

1) Choose a pilot area to work on.
2) Separate internal and external activities. Another good use of SMED is to improve meeting time. A meeting that includes several team members, including managers, should be reduced to the minimum (internal tasks), while all the rest of the time is spent individually in preparation and reporting, tasks that you will call "external."
3) What steps require downtime, and which ones do not? For example, what do you do when your printer needs the ink changed?
4) Cut out the Waste or eliminate non-essential operations. Lean it out. Example: "I should only touch this once in the shutdown."
5) Parallel changeovers. Many hands make light work, as long as the shutdown time is not costing you more than the production time. Example: Like the speed of a self-organized pit crew changing four tires.
6) Add power to your change-over. Do this check at the end, so you cannot make external activities faster in the shutdown. Example: Vacuum is faster than a broom, an impact wrench is faster than hand tools.

Steps to improve SMED

1) Observe and document the current process – "AS IS"
2) Categorize the activities as Internal (done during the changeover) or External (tasks that can be executed before or after)

3) Identify which Internal steps can be external
4) Create flow with the remaining internal activities
5) Create flow / optimize the external activities
6) Document the new process, so it's repeatable and reproducible
7) Never stop improving

Spaghetti Diagram

A spaghetti diagram is a visual representation using a continuous flow line tracing the path of an item or activity through a process. The continuous flow line enables process teams to identify redundancies in the workflow and opportunities to expedite process flow.[32]

How to implement it with 5S

You can use it with 5S to identify the best location for an item. If used frequently, it should be stored near where it is needed.

Spaghetti diagram benefits
- Reduced delays: it helps to highlight major intersection points within a room. Where many walk paths overlap may cause delays.
- Reduced footprint and wasted movement of people, products and information.
- Better ergonomics

Steps to implement the Spaghetti Diagram[33]

- Identify the process that needs to be improved
- Collect required resources (like floor plan, color pencils or markers, stopwatch, team, operators, flip charts, measuring tape etc.,)

---

[32] The Public Health Quality Improvement Handbook. Ron Bialek, Grace L. Duffy, and John W. Moran

[33] Extracted from **https://sixsigmastudyguide.com/spaghetti-diagram/**

- Draw the layout of the process on paper scaling down to match the distance between each work point includes all the equipment, walls, machinery, bins etc.
- Draw the path of the process from start to ending, following the movement of each employee continuously from beginning to end of the process
- Draw each movement between two locations with a continuous line. Use a different line for each movement.
- Use different color pencils or markers to capture different employees or material movements
- Measure the time or distance of each path, the number of hand-offs, shifts, operator and other related information.
- Create a new diagram showing the process's ideal state that reduces the walking time or eliminates the non-value-added activities.

ACHIEVING CULTURAL CHANGE

"Culture is what we do. It isn't an HR job. It's everyone's job"

Luciana Paulise

5S implementations help to develop new habits. When employees change their habits, they are impacting the company culture. People tend to get back to old habits, almost unconsciously. Therefore, you may see some changes in the first months, but if there isn't a system to help everyone involved sustain the new habits, you get back to square one. Cultural change doesn't happen. Below you will learn the steps to sustain the implementation to achieve cultural change, a long-term transformation.

Culture simply said, is what people do when nobody is looking. Culture includes common behaviors and habits that the company value and respect that helps employees make decisions and achieve results aligned with the company's purpose. Once you have the right habits ingrained in your employees, all you need to do is hire new employees, let them know the company's purpose, and make sure they meet other teams to get the culture by example.

A cultural change is a change in those habits or behaviors in people's daily routines. Cultural transformation can be intentional or defined by new company circumstances that drive new habits.

Is the implementation being sustained?
Cultural change is hard, as it takes time to align everyone to a common purpose. That's why it is particularly difficult to say you failed in the 5s implementation. Maybe the organization just flipped the page

too quickly. Cultural change takes at least two years to be sustained through time.

How can you be sure your 5S implementation is being sustained? The first signs are:

- Contractors, suppliers and customers visiting the facility are surprised; they note the change and talk about it.
- Employees are proud of the change and want to showcase their progress; they are not afraid of audits as there is nothing to hide. On the contrary, they want to show off improvements.
- Employees want to keep learning about the tool and ask when is the next class
- Teams that have not been part of the implementation yet want to take the training class. They have seen advanced teams' success, engagement and joy.
- 1S and 2S findings are rare in audits; old habits of not cleaning after yourself or leaving tools unattended are way behind while new habits have taken place.
- Employees don't stop their production process to do 5S; 5S is part of the process.

If this is not happening, the new culture is not in place yet. How can you make the culture change happen?

Why are 5S implementations hard to sustain?

Many companies started to implement 5S just to realize it doesn't stick through time easily.

Today, most businesses understand the importance of cleanliness and organization to achieve performance excellence. Still, most of them just see it as a show-off tool, not as part of the company's culture. So everyone has to clean "for a visit."

Some companies even start with their own employees as trainers because 5S is simple to understand. Many of these companies begin vigorously, then six months later, the effort drowns. And they start over again five years later. For some reason, it doesn't stick quickly. They all find it difficult to achieve the desired long-term results of self-discipline, safety, continuous maintenance and employee engagement.

This trend was found even across different countries and cultures. 90% of the companies interviewed had started 5S implementation at least twice in the past.

5S cannot be implemented in a one-day or one-week 5S event. Employees will not implement it organically only by learning the concepts. They need to practice them every single day. 5S has to become part of their work. 5S steps have to be ingrained in their daily processes, everywhere they go, even when nobody is looking.

5s rules are helpful everywhere: in your workstation, your partner's workstation, in the break room or the bathroom. Once you start enjoying the benefits of applying 5S, you respect the rules everywhere. The keys to success are:

1)   Reinforce the 5S microsteps across all the organizational levels continuously, through an extended period, a minimum of two years, to apply the tool every day, all the time, to achieve a sustained change.

2)   Build an environment that is fertile for cultural change. HR and the leadership team will work together to enable cultural change.

3)   Follow a disciplined approach to change management company-wide.

12 steps to manage culture change

To enable the cultural change company-wide, the leadership team will partner with other roles or departments such as HR (Human Resources), PR (Public relations), Chief Culture Officers and Maintenance, depending on each case. It's a cross-functional effort. Change needs to be acknowledged, mapped, and communicated to everyone.

People need to be coached and guided to achieve the change (this is crucial; it won't happen just because someone says it's a good change). There must be a disciplined, but at the same time, agile system to guide change management. Below you will learn about the MMM method with three stages: Map the change, manage people, and master continuous innovation (see image 42).

The MMM is divided into 12 steps to complement your operational efforts to make 5S stick through a cultural change. While the five steps Sort, Store, Shine, Standardize and Self-organize drive behavioral change within a team, the MMM strives to support and align those team behaviors at the company level.

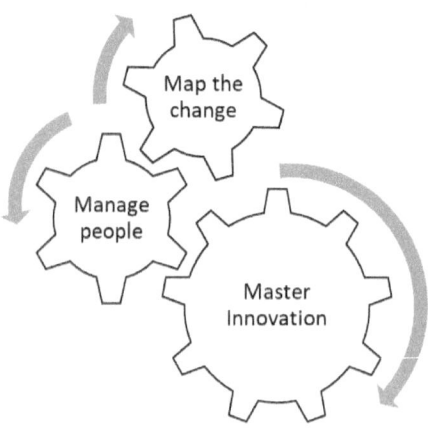

Image 42

Map the change

The first stage, map the change, focus on planning and setting the stage for the change. It includes picturing an engaging purpose, defining ground rules, mapping the process, clear goals and clear responsibilities.

1) **Picture an Engaging Purpose:**

Change is not easy, so people need a strong reason to change. Just because "it will help the company make more money," it is not a reason to engage everyone. Companies need to think of a more compelling story that can drive behaviors. A good example of a purpose is Dr. Reddy's[34]. It is a 33-year-old global pharmaceutical company in India that produces affordable generic medication with more than 20,000 employees. Unfortunately, decision-making and procedures became too complex over the years.

Prasad, the CEO sought to evolve Dr. Reddy's culture to be innovative and patient-centered, so he decided to search for PURPOSE. They came up with: "Good health can't wait." After the idea of "good health can't wait," was introduced, one of the scientists developed a product in 15 days, something unthinkable in the healthcare industry. That's the power of a clear purpose.

2) **Define Ground rules**

It is essential to define standard ground rules for everybody to align how you want 5S to become a part of your work. Ground rules define what is acceptable and what Is not during the change; they are like a Manifesto. Basic ground rules should be no more than 12 and could be some currently used by the company if any available or specific for the project. Some examples are being a team player, aiming for excellence, or being kind to the environment. They will provide a scope for the teams to ensure alignment and commitment.

Suppose the company or team you are implementing doesn't have clear values. In that case, you can meet first to define them, or you can simply use the CARE values: **connect** to the 5S purpose, **attend and ask** questions, **respect** everyone and everything, and **empower** others.

Why are these rules so important? Because they help to make decisions and guide behaviors. For example, when I deliver the 5S training, we visit section by section with the entire team. All the team

---

[34] https://hbr.org/2017/06/changing-company-culture-requires-a-movement-not-a-mandate

members see each other's mess (or organization). Commonly, they laugh at what they find and blame one another. I always remind them, "Remember the value RESPECT." Or they say it is not my job to decide where to put the tools or how to clean, why would I do it? And I say, "because you are EMPOWERED to do so now." These values are not only cold statements; they must be demonstrated with behaviors at the leadership level to have an impact. If the leaders don't respect the rules of the section they are visiting, they are breaking these values; therefore, employees will do the same.

3) Map the process and the risks

Mapping the process is about providing a guide to help the employees build the right habits. 5S urges people to become self-organized so that everyone does their job, exposes barriers to achieve it, and strives to solve them. The first microstep is "Sort needed from unneeded." What is it that bothers them, that makes them work more or makes them feel unsafe? Employees need a process to report or remove what is not required in the workplace.

The process can be: when you find an item that is not needed, remove it or fill in an action plan to remove it later. If the item that needs removal is an asset, you can define a process to red tag it when it is over a certain threshold to ensure it is approved first. You can map communication routines, reporting routines, cleaning routines, and daily or weekly team routines to know how to support the 5S training.

Risks also need to be mapped and analyzed before starting the implementation. You can do an FMEA (Failure mode and effect analysis, see FMEA TOOLS TO COMPLEMENT 5S) or ask your team questions like the following:

- How is productivity going to be impacted during the 5S implementation? How is it going to be handled? 5S takes time as employees need to organize their workstations and define new routines. Audits, courses and walkarounds are also time-consuming. Not taking this into account could delay the implementation. At first, 5S reduces productivity while being implemented until it becomes part of the work, and it starts improving productivity.
- Which teams or processes need to start implementing first to create a significant impact?
- Is taking pictures allowed? I usually recommend taking photos and videos to help define standards and before and after pictures. For

example, some companies only let auditors and trainers take pictures, others only allow leaders, and some don't allow photos.

#	DATE	SECTION	FINDING	WHAT NEEDS TO BE DONE	WHO	ESTIMATED CLOSING	PROGRESS %	
	1-31-19	CM-3	AIR GUN	HOME FOR AIR GUN	M-A	2-29-19	90%	
	1-31-19	CM-3	PPE	PPE NEEDS HOME	M-A	2-29-19	90%	
	1-31-19	CM-3	CHAIR	NEEDS HOME	M-A	2-29-19	50%	
	1-31-19	CM-3	AIR FILTERS	Change more often	Maint		50%	
	4-22-19	CM-3	Payoff	NEW Paint	M-A		95%	
	4-22-19	CM-3	Top and Bottom Hold Down	New Paint	M-A		50%	
	5-14-19	CM-3	w/wall AUXILIARY	Home	M-A			6:
	6-4-19	CM-3	Payoff Arms	NEEDS HOME	M-A	7-5-19	60% 100%	6:
	6-22-19	CM-3	Timer	Needs Home	M-A	6-27-19	100%	6-

Image 43 – Action Plan

4) Clear roles and responsibilities

Everyone in the company should be involved in the 5S effort. Every area and every object needs an owner. A way to ensure no gray areas is to use a company map and divide it into physical sections with owners. No matter the size, what matters is that every employee gets to be the owner of a small piece of land, which may include equipment, floor, walls, tools, procedures, etc.

5) Clear Goals

Managers or in self-organizing teams, the employees, should set clear goals for their sections. This goal should be published for everyone to see; transparency is key to cascading the good results and the lessons learned to other company areas. Examples of clear goals are the number of training sessions, the number of action items/improvements per month per section or the 5S audit score. If there is a scorecard already, 5S metrics should be included.

Manage people
6) Deliver company-wide training

To empower (CARE – E for empower) your employees, you need to train them and give them the tools they need to succeed. Start the implementation with a pilot team,

- Provide a 5S introductory training to everyone associated with the company: employees, contractors, customers, security, maintenance or safety.

- Specific management training is ideal for helping leaders transition to self-organization. Leaders should not tell employees what to do, but employees should detect the issues to work on and organize their time to solve them.

- If a contractor is in charge of the 5S implementation, it is recommended to organize a train the trainer session to keep the knowledge in-house and ensure continuity through time.

- HR can also be trained to communicate 5S within and outside the company. HR's job is to support the implementation throughout the entire employee experience (recruiting, hiring, onboarding, engaging, performing, developing and departing).

- The most critical part of the training is hands-on implementation. Employees need to see onsite how 5S helps them. You can do walkarounds to teach them how to inspect workstations to remove unneeded items, identify items with no home, gray areas, empty cabinets, or leaks. Practice how to fill the Action Plan or cleaning schedule features. Remember, "common sense is the least common of the senses," so employees need to learn to see dirt, leaks, or issues in general with a positive mindset focus on solving them all through time. I usually do specific hands-on training sessions for one S at a time to start small.

- Training on other continuous improvement tools: SMED, FMEA, 5 why's, and TPM are the typical tools that employees will find useful during a 5S Implementation. You learn more about them in the TOOLS TO COMPLEMENT 5S Chapter.

7) Monitor and share results through external audits

Organize monthly internal or external reviews to monitor results to provide a good status report and feedback to the employees of what needs to be 5S. Share audits in whiteboards or shared spaces for everyone to see, and include pictures and detailed comments for each section. Employees can use audit findings as action items for their action plans.

8) Test and replicate

5S implementation can start with a pilot team to practice. Fail, and try as needed to map the most effective implementation process, and then replicate the success to the other groups. Starting with a pilot also helps to showcase how a 5S workplace looks and sets common standards for colors, labels, and other communications tools. This pilot team will become your snow-ball effect starter; whatever they do will be contagious. And they will be able to teach others, which is also a part of building self-organizing teams: decentralizing information.

9) Over-communicate

Communicate the 5S process through the values, principles and microsteps and results in every possible format, such as meetings, newsletters, emails, minutes, flyers, blogs or Slack channels.

Teams can showcase before and after pictures o boards with the audit results.

It's ok to feel you are over-communicating, though it is never too much.

The other essential communication plan is within the team. You can create a communication routine to share 5S information daily within the group, or from shift to shift. An example of this routine could be a 5-minute 5S topic in every team meeting, a 15-minute standup meeting at the end of the shifts, or a monthly meeting to share the audit results. (See 5S CONCEPTS – Team Routines).

10) Coach

Based on the audit results, you can identify performance trends. Use them to coach the teams that are outliers or behind schedule. Don't punish them. It is most likely there is a problem with the leaders, the team structure, or the implementation process is not adequate for them. Sometimes continuous processes like in a manufacturing setting, the kitchen of a restaurant or a hospital OR don't allow for free time to work on 5S. Set specific time-slots to work on 5S. It is hard for leaders and team members to become self-organized. Employees traditionally learn to follow orders and avoid asking questions. It takes time to shift from command and control to self-organizing and making decisions, but it is not impossible. Work closely with the team to figure out what they need. Provide them with a team coach or facilitator to help them accelerate the implementation.

Master change and innovation

11) Kudos: Reward the team effort

Once a team achieves a decent level of organization, how can you motivate them to continue improving? Positive reinforcement is one of the ways. Being proud is another option. Team members that understand the benefits of 5S feel proud of what they have accomplished. They see the results and positively impact their daily activities, making it easier to work every day.

Rewards are not always money-based or expansive. When employees feel joy and pride for their work, a thank-you note, a hand-shake or even the possibility to help other teams is a reward: an intrinsic motivator. If you just give money, an extrinsic motivator, it helps for sure, but it is only a short-term carrot and stick tool. It is like giving money to your kid for doing great at school, it just doesn't sound right, and it is not sustainable through time. The team members will only work if there is a possibility of getting extra money.

Intrinsic motivators instead are long-term. Employees respect the processes even if nobody is looking. They want to continue to feel in control and proud of themselves. Self-organization has the power to achieve intrinsic motivation.

Some ideas are:

- Team dinners or breakfasts
- Certificates or badges for training sessions or audit scores achieved
- Development opportunities, like training other team members in 5S
- Showing team improvements to other facilities and being showcased in newsletters
- Sending Thank you card signed by the company president
- Inviting family members to see the improvements

It is crucial for the success of the rewards that it is clear why they are receiving them. A simple thank you with no specifics doesn't motivate. Be as specific as possible, describing what has been accomplished. Team members need to know what exactly is that you want to reinforce. Like with kids, the most valuable thing you give team members is your time. Show them that you spent time reviewing what they did.

Team rewards are better than individual rewards so that the team members don't compete against each other. Some companies like

Zappos, 1800 Contacts or Globant, do peer-rewards, which are adequate to bring more fairness to the process. Team members choose to reward a co-worker because they have seen them doing a great job.

Whatever reward you offer, make it something you can sustain. And especially, align the type of "bonus" with the other groups in the committee meeting to ensure fairness across the groups.

12) **Support people for continuous innovation**

The last but not least piece to sustain 5S is to develop a system that sets people free to innovate continuously as a way of working. One of the first reasons 5S doesn't stick easily is that employees get tired of asking for resources from leaders without even getting an answer. If you want your team to change, be part of it. Go to the *gemba* (the workstations, where the action takes place in Japanese) to see what's going on. Give them time and resources. Follow-up on their improvements as a way to show support.

Leaders need to reinforce 5S every day, especially walking the talk. If you see a piece of paper on the floor, pick it up. Clean your table when you leave. Be the first to implement 5S in your office or section and set a precedent for the employees.

Work with HR to help 5S be part of the employee experience, including 5S content in the hiring interviews, the onboarding package, the development curricula, and even as part of the contractor's safety training.

Some ideas for showing support for continuous innovation are:

- Visit other companies (Toyota plants usually offer a free tour to see how their facilities implement The Toyota Production System and 5S)
- Benchmark other teams or other locations within your company
- Visit clients and suppliers or invite them to visit and ask them for feedback
- Organize cross-functional training sessions, where you include members from different teams to agree on standards or shared processes.
- Schedule 5S days

As 5S drives cultural change, results include improved employee engagement, reduction in safety incidents, improved productivity and better quality. And the reason why all these results are accomplished is that employees have changed their behaviors. There is no need to control; they are autonomous and self-organized. When they find a problem, they try to correct it immediately or report it. They clean more often and even avoid machines or workspaces from getting dirty by working more consciously. They organize their tools before leaving the shift. They are proud of their workspace, increasing their willingness to participate in improvement projects. When behaviors change across different sectors, change spreads faster, introducing a cultural change. And the best sign of cultural change is employees' reaction to audits. At first, they were hiding issues. They didn't care that much about the audit results; they just didn't want to get more work to do. When employees want to be audited, they are ready to showcase their improvements and already have in mind what they want to work on for the following review. A cultural change has occurred.

Implementing 5S as a branding strategy

While companies have been focusing on the customer experience for a long time, now it's time to also focus on the "employee experience." Employees have now become customers of the workplace. Employees are no longer ready to leave their personal lives aside for a job or expect to keep the same job for 20 years. In the Era of Knowledge, employees make the company special, and they know it, so they want to choose where to work and how, or else, they simply fly away. They decide to be part of a company based on the purpose, brand and culture. As per Gallup's research[35] , one in three employees strongly agrees with the statement, "The mission and purpose of my organization make me feel my job is important."

Companies that turn the ratio to eight in ten achieve a 51% reduction in absenteeism, a 64% drop in safety incidents and a 29% improvement in quality.

Compared with all other workers, Disengaged workers report more days of work missed (3.5 more days per person per year) and more days of work missed for illness (0.55 days per person). The lower productivity of actively disengaged workers penalizes the US economy for 300 billion dollars[36] per year due to disengagement.

Purpose, brand and culture are key to boosting the employee experience. That is why many companies are directing their efforts to use their culture as a branding strategy.

Certain cultural behaviors can easily be spotted as good or bad in a company just by doing a short walk around. Colorful workstations, open spaces, round tables, in-company restaurants, information boards, multiple common areas, and groups of employees informally chatting are usually signs of team-oriented cultures. Some companies like Google or Zappos use their culture to brand the companies to hire the best employees: they show the beautiful restaurants in the facilities, the mini golfs, swimming pools, relax stations, or even the parties they organize. It is part of who they are and why they are successful.

---

[35] https://www.gallup.com/workplace/242252/employee-experience.aspx

[36]   https://news.gallup.com/businessjournal/439/what-your-disaffected-workers-cost.aspx

GE and Toyota were among the first companies to use quality and workplace organization to brand their companies. Likewise, you can use 5S to help your company visually stand out from other competitors.

5S is a visual help to align strategy (what you think) with the brand (what you say) with the culture (what you do).

The way 5S changes how a workplace look is so impressive that any visitor who has been previously at the plant can notice a difference. The before-after pictures, the audit comments posted on the boards, or the labels and signs help even more to highlight how a company can change from the bottom-up.

Benefits of using the 5S as a branding strategy

There are various benefits of using culture as a branding strategy:

- Employees become our brand ambassadors, reducing training and hiring costs. They even recommend the company to their friends.
- Customers become brand ambassadors: customers can recognize the value of our company. 5s becomes a sign of quality and organization, so they feel comfortable recommending the company to others.
- There is a virtuous cycle for which employees and managers feel proud about their 5S brand, so they boost efforts to continue making it better through time. This is because 5S implementation never ends; change is continuous and contagious and gets stronger through time.

5S is more than a tool; it is a culture itself. Using 5S as a branding strategy helps companies build stronger bonds with their customers, suppliers, employees, and even their employees' families, showing long-term commitment and setting an example for others to imitate.

Commons myths

"5s is just another tool."

It is not just the flavor of the month, 5S implementation may take up to 2 years to drive culture change. 5S sticks when all team members are trained to think differently, and leaders set the example. After several days, you can see behavioral changes, but they are not sustained if the 12 change management steps are not followed thoroughly. Ensure training courses are available for new hires, contractors and leaders, continuously updating standards, team routines are in place and consistent communication strategy.

"I don't have time to do 5S".

Yes, 5S takes time, but you set your own schedule and action plan. Time to implement it should be planned from the beginning to allow employees to stop working and sorting. Once training is over, 5S shouldn't mean extra work. Actually, 5S implementation increases efficiency and reduces time wasted in other activities that don't add value, so you have more time to clean and store your tools. You don't stop working to do 5S. You do 5S as part of your job. You do 5S when you use a tool and store it back right after using it. You do 5S when you run out of inventory and immediately coordinate the replenishment based on the visual system designed.

"5S is for the front-line workers."

5S is implemented by the front-line workers, but also by the admins, by the leaders, by the contractors. 5S is for everyone. Everyone should be on board. Especially top management. They need to be involved from the very beginning to provide guidance, provide resources, prioritize, ensure issues are being followed-up, show the purpose and be the example. Their desks should be the cleanest and most organized.

"We can't focus on 5S now; productivity is our priority".

5S is a way to stay more productive. It helps reduce wasted time, wasted inventory, and other resources. It also reduces mistakes as people learn to eliminate distractions and focus more on the current task. Problems are detected earlier in the process before they get worse, reducing re-works, mistakes, safety incidents and customer complaints. 5S is like planning; you plan to fail if you don't plan. If you don't spend time on 5S before, you will fix problems later.

APPENDIX I:

5S CASE STUDIES BY INDUSTRY

"5S your life."

5S was initially implemented in manufacturing, but many other industries discovered its benefits through time. No matter where you apply it, you will find it useful. At home, at school, at the church, everywhere you go. That's why it is recommended to engage the entire company in implementing 5S.

The following are examples of implementations in different settings.

5S in Manufacturing

5S was implemented in an international bottling company throughout all the sectors, including its suppliers, to reduce costs, increase engagement, and improve safety.

They defined the 5S methodology as a fundamental part of its growth and sustainable development. We worked with them to implement 5S at the bottling lines, the manufacturing sector, administration, the dining room, the first aid room, and even the entry and security area. Also, suppliers were trained. Why did they choose this tool? How did they benefit from it?

With the 5S steps, sort, store, shine, standardize, and self-organize, they seek to align the objectives of the different sectors of the organization by applying new habits and behaviors. With a clear definition of responsibilities and processes established visually, it is possible to improve the communication between the sectors and eliminate the "gray areas" where no one takes full accountability. It seems like a simple tool since it does not use statistics like Six Sigma, nor does it require prior knowledge. However, it is challenging to implement it because it requires a cultural change.

That's why the first thing we did was implement the first S, sort: divide the entire organization into sectors, both physically and in terms of personnel, and choose a pilot sector with which to start training.

1S - Sort

As part of the first S, sort, we defined which tools or documents were needed and which were not. We prepared an inventory. Many tools and objects did not correspond to the sector, or too many of them. One of the first exercises was to check the employee's toolboxes, one by one, object by object, to define what was needed. The toolboxes contained lots of duplicated tools and broken items; it was impossible to keep track of them. And, of course, the toolbox was super heavy. By taking out the tools that were not needed in the area (maybe they brought from areas where they previously worked), and removing duplicated and broken items, the toolbox could be replaced with a smaller one. They even built foam separators and an inventory sheet to be able to recognize what was missing before finishing work. See the images below.

One of the characteristics of 5S is just to work with the people's ideas. The workers themselves expressed what they needed and what they didn't need. Sometimes they do not know how to talk about it, do not find who to tell, or are afraid to provide their feedback.

5S doesn't look forward to blaming but expects ownership. The idea is to make sure that problems are highlighted, not hidden. The only way to do that is by eliminating fear. 5S especially supports transparency by emphasizing visual management.

Image 44 – Before 5S

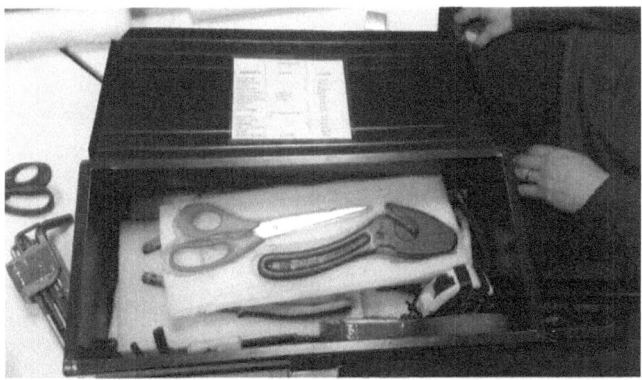

Image 45 – After 5S

2 S - Store

As part of the second S, we continued doing walkthroughs. Although we had already eliminated many things, it was challenging to maintain the workplace organized. The employees did not agree to identify shelves or tools, "we all know where to find it; we have been working here for many years." But, new employees or suppliers were the leading cause of chaos and disorder, and it was difficult to avoid it. By identifying what they needed and defining a specific place to locate, everyone (including contractors and suppliers) would find it and store it back after using it. In advance, team members defined how many they needed of each element and when they needed to do the replenishment. They also considered the weight of the object, the distance to the actual place of use, the frequency of use, and its size to choose the most suitable and safest place.

3 S - Shine

Cleaning the objects after being used is essential to keep them always "as brand-new," which is the beginning of the third S, Shine. A lot of money is spent maintaining unneeded stock or replacing and repairing. Proper maintenance is a better preventive action. As part of the 3S, cleaning schedules for each sector and its instruments were defined. From the roof and the windows, the machinery, tools, and drawers through the floor. 5S in industries seeks not to clean but to avoid getting dirty in the first place.

The A-Ha moment was to realize the team members should be working together with the contractors in charge of cleaning, defining real cleaning schedules, measuring the needed times, and assigning responsibilities to the operators, like avoiding getting dirty. How do we avoid that? By eliminating sources of dirt, such as broken cables, machines, windows, or doors. Also, looking for the root causes that generated the dust was part of their work. And finally, they identified those places that were hard to access. Maybe they were floors covered by boxes, hidden storage sectors, or inaccessible and inconspicuous sectors.

4 S - Standardize

The first 3 S's changed enormously how the operators worked and how the plant looked like. After some time, instead of blaming someone, everyone was looking for solutions. Even suppliers and external auditors were astonished by the change. But some groups left 5S aside over time due to lack of time or personnel changes. They needed to increase the visibility of the norms to make them "unforgettable." The bottling company began to apply visual controls everywhere, defined procedures, and added 5S standards to current processes. The systems should be clear for everyone. They included pictures, sketches, checklists, and videos. Not only do they have to say what has to be done, but how, when, and by whom. They were very specific and detailed.

5S – Self-organize

And before implementing the fifth S is where many companies abandoned. This company though, focused on a long-term implementation from the very beginning. We started with a diagnostic and continued with monthly audits to all the sections for years. They also continued to train new hires, leaders and even visitors to ensure everyone was aligned.

Benefits
Some of the benefits obtained throughout the company were:

- Higher productivity and fewer delays
- Increased productivity levels and fewer delays, even during a turnaround
- Improved employee morale, engagement and teamwork
- reduced waste on the floor and inside cabinets
- optimized use of space
- Improved safety by moving items located in inadequate places or reducing hazards
- Enhanced detection of water, oil and product leaks
- Enforced ownership of all articles and all areas
- improved equipment maintenance
- improved inventory management and retrieval time

5S in Accommodation and food service activities

5S is a methodology to improve employee involvement, reduce waste, organize the workflow, and reduce safety hazards, so why not apply it to the kitchen.

Applying 5S to restaurants helps reduce wait time and prevent errors. These two factors are vital to increasing customer satisfaction and ensuring high profitability by quick tables turnover.

To achieve these improvements, each restaurant area was subject to 5S: the kitchen, the salon, the hostess desk, the drive-thru area, the bathrooms, the storage area. And every element should be sorted, stored in the right place at the right time with the right amount, and look like new. Always. Here is how we did it:

1 S - Sort
The kitchen and storage areas should only contain what is needed to avoid cross-contamination. We assigned owners to all the areas, including restrooms, storage locations, kitchen, change rooms etc. Employees looked for elements that were out of place, broken, dirty or past due. Kitchens usually have limited space, so removing what is not needed is important to leave the space for what is required more often.

They also analyzed each ingredient and tool's frequency of use and then sorted them out based on the findings.

Kitchens tend to be a place where everything is stored, as it is the only part the customer doesn't have access to. Remember not to organize for a visit, but for your team. In this case, the kitchen was an "open style" similar to the one in the image below, so it was an even stronger reason to keep everything neat.

Image 46

Everything needed to be in the right place. Restaurants typically have lots of decoration, which makes them very colorful indeed, but through time, those pictures, ornaments and wreaths may deteriorate. Employees worked hard to remove or fix items that were not in good condition and made sure they were clean.

2 S - Store
Everything needed to be organized and stored to be found easily in less than 30 seconds. Labels, containers and color codes were used to help remember the right place for everything and consider dating products so that FIFO (first in, first out) stock rotation could be quickly followed.

You also need to consider which items you want the customer to see and which you don't. The first step is to organize items considering placing the most frequently used items nearest their doors or the heaviest in an easy-access place. For example, table cleaners and menus should be placed close to the hostess desk, but be careful! Table cleaners can contaminate food or deteriorate the menu, so keep them separate and especially keep the cleaner away from the customer view. Improving storing location reduces movement and enhances communication, saving time and misunderstandings.

3S - Shine

All areas should be clean at all times. Employees cannot wait until lunchtime is over to start cleaning. Employees should live by the motto's keep it brand-new and leave it the same way you receive it. So if the floor is dirty, no matter which floor, you don't wait till the cleaning staff is available, you clean it right away, to avoid falls and contamination to other areas. A cleaning schedule is an excellent tool, but it is not enough. Bathrooms and open kitchens get real nasty in rush hour, so team members don't need to wait till a customer gets to see the mess.

Lots of restaurants have lousy restrooms during the last hour of service. Even if there is only one customer, service and cleanliness should remain excellent and at all times. It's about changing employee habits. If they simply follow the cleaning schedule, they will not clean during the last hour.

4S - Standardize

The standardize phase is key to keeping the first three steps up and running through time. First, employees took pictures of the "ideal look" for every room, table, or storage area so that it was easy to keep it always the same way. Next, they prepared checklists and schedules that included the WHO, WHAT, HOW and WHEN.

Every item should have a standard, from floors to ceilings, tables to plates, and waiters to owner clothes. Visual aids and clear responsibilities make it easier to maintain the organization. Make sure every place and item has an owner, and that owner knows how to keep it organized. Use visual management tools to make communication easier. Cookers and servers may speak different languages, so signs like pictures, diagrams, colors and labels help to build a universal language.

5 – Self-organize

5s can only be sustained with everybody's help. Train the whole team with the 5S methodology and have everybody responsible for a part of the restaurant. Restaurants suffer a high turnover rate, so keep training a priority to ensure everyone is on board.

Furthermore, make everyone part of the change: everything that is used needs to be returned to the same place where it was. Every label or instruction must be followed, and every error must be communicated. The self-organize phase is achieved when every employee is self-disciplined enough to sustain what has been agreed upon. To ensure this happens, schedule periodic audits to review the different areas. Sometimes only outsiders can see the real mess.

5S in Administrative and support service activities

5S is also helpful in an office environment. There was an office where the amount of paperwork and the time spent to retrieve was a complete waste of time and money and a headache, of course. If an audit came, you needed to retrieve documents from 3 years ago or more (remember that accounting paperwork like invoices usually requires to be kept for ten years for tax or legal reasons), and you had to do it fast.

What happened is that each team and every analyst would store documents their way. Some were careful and included many details in each folder, while others were highly plain and included too little information. In the end, documentation was hard to be found and costly because they had older boxes in offsite storage. If you needed to bring them back and forth quickly (usually the standard service took around three days, but if you needed them fast, it was an extra cost), the expense was higher.

1S and 2S - Sort and store
5S helped organize the paperwork, categorizing each type of documentation based on the team who produced it, the kind of documentation, the month and year, and the estimated retrieval frequency. That categorization would tell the user where to store the documents, how to label them, and when they should be moved to another storage location. It was pretty automated and error-free because we had uploaded the categories to a database, so every time you would enter the type of document to print the label, it would help you fill it with pre-entered information. If it were a current document, you would store it at your desk, if it were x months old, you would store it in the shared area drawers, and if it were older than a year, you would store it offsite. Every drawer was labeled indicating the customer/plant, the month and the year. We had calculated how much space we needed each month based on historical data, so we know exactly how many months we had on-site. Having that information, team members also re-distributed the

shared area drawers accordingly so that groups with more documents would have more space available.

With the amount and type of documents well defined, it was hard for outliers not to meet the requirements or deadlines because it was easy to tell. They would run out of space anyway, and folders would be on their desk or over the floor, exposing waste and errors.

3S - Shine
Then there was a routine for cleaning the desk every day before leaving and keeping unfinished documents locked in a temporary folder or drawers. Even though there was specific personnel for doing the regular clean-up, **team members would make sure their desk and drawers were clean at all times,** as visitors would come often and sometimes without notice.

4S - Standardize
There was a "filing day" every month or every three months (depending on the number of documents every group generated). It was coordinated in advance with the filing room and the rest of the teams. Everyone would clean their desk and move documents out to the common area and from the common area to the filing room. For example, if the schedule were every three months, all the team members in a specific section would move the same three months out to the other location, so everybody knew which period of documentation was on–site anytime.

Standardization in an office, especially with repetitive tasks, is essential. Standardization of documents, naming conventions, ownership of computers helps to improve communication, as long as it doesn't get too bureaucratic.

5S – Self-organize
The best part of the project was that they were not only able to retrieve faster and easier documentation within your team. If you were moved to another department, they had implemented the same system, so everyone knew how to organize and find documents everywhere in the company.

The team developed a refresher training every three months to train new hires.

They also performed periodic audits in which, for example, they chose to retrieve random documents. They would double-check if the content and labels were correct according to the description and see if they were stored in the right place. They conducted walkthroughs in the early morning or late afternoon to ensure cleanliness or identify classified documents left unlocked. If things were out of place, they would leave a tag or fill a report to make sure they were well aware of something wrong.

5S in Transportation and storage

5S was also useful in a transportation company. With my team, we implemented 5S, starting with the workshop in the worst condition and generating more delays to the trucks transporting oil and gas. Then my team continued with the administration and then with the traffic sector. If you had visited the company before, you would indeed be surprised after 5S; you wouldn't have recognized it!

The impact of 5S

Each employee started to notify if a tool was damaged or if a machine was not working. Before 5S, they would accept the failure and move on. If the previous shift did not meet the standard, the boss was not notified, the same employees helped each other to respect the processes. They alone started to solve the root cause of the problems, not waiting for the boss to bring all the answers. And above all, together, they maintained order and cleanliness, reducing delays, work times, errors and preventing accidents.

1S - Sort

The first step was to separate needed from unneeded. The usefulness of an object has to do with how it is used and where. Different locations have different standards. Some items were useful in one place but not in another. For example, a damaged tire was not valuable in the workshop; it needed to be separated from the good tires to avoid confusion. But it had to be sorted out and marked for later repair. You couldn't confuse a new part with a broken one; it could represent a safety incident or a delay when used by the truck driver.

Every square foot of the workshop was assigned to someone. Every part and every location had an owner. The person in charge had to define what was needed in that place. Some items were expired, deteriorated, or not used in the area in the next 12 months. They had to be removed, sent to another sector, sold or repaired.

Each employee had to be aware of their surroundings and ensure that only required items were found. The useless ones only took up space, generated dirt and were a source of errors.

2S - Store

Once the not useful items were separated, they were organized for ease of use and to reduce search time. The way to maintain a place for the things was to identify the "home" with labels, posters, drawings or photos so that anyone could see if it was located correctly. For example, in the workshop, a tool board was rearranged so that the silhouettes of the tools were visible. Employees could quickly notice the absence of any item.

3S - Shine

Employees had to make sure supplies and tools were looking brand-new. That is, clean and in good condition, suitable for use or sale. We couldn't afford to delay the departure of a truck because we had parts in poor condition.

Shine involves having the necessary elements to clean appropriately, defining a calendar to maintain cleanliness and, above all, "avoid dirt." Some sources of dirt and dust can be removed by avoiding opening windows or not eating in the work sector but having a specific industry for it.

Employees created a cleaning kit to keep handy so that if dirt was generated, it could be cleaned immediately. As part of cleaning, one of the first rules was to place the snacks in the cabinets in specific places for their conservation, where you could avoid contaminating other elements with crumbs and odors.

4S- Standardize

The standardize phase was about creating a "system" that allowed us to maintain the three S. The team developed a procedure with an inventory and how items should be stored and kept clean. One way to standardize was to use photos, checklists, or calendars to help staff remember their responsibilities.

5S- Self-organize

Just as 5S seems very easy to apply, it is easy to forget if efforts are not sustained.

The team started to be audited by us to comply with the standards. We were doing external 5S audits every three months to assess the evolution of the methodology and help propose new action plans. The hardest part of the implementation was complying to respect what was defined all the time, with no exceptions. The key was to teach them to repeat, repeat and repeat the new habits.

Like riding a bike, you never forget it once you learn the system.

5S in Wholesale and Retail

My team and I implemented 5S in several retail stores, from selling home appliances and furniture to beauty salons and clothes apparel.

The impact of 5S

5S impacted reducing costs, improving the traffic inside the store, reducing retrieving time, and improving employee and customer satisfaction. The client saw the changes in the retail stores as the products were in better condition, clean and more visible. The storage locations were also re-organized. Even when the customer could not see them, the results impacted suppliers and employees.

1S – Sort

I remember the first time I got into one of the AC storage locations. Boxes were stored unsafely; broken equipment was mixed with good equipment. They were looking forward to moving to a bigger place.

First, employees scanned what they wanted to remove if they were damaged or unfit for sale. Some were clearly not unfit for use, but employees said they needed to contact the owner to see if he wanted to keep them. So the next step was to define the rules of what was considered needed and unneeded in terms of 5S. The third step was to agree to empower the employees to decide to remove items based on those rules and avoid second-guessing.

The other big problem was to make sure all the items were in stock. Many units were not on the system; some were duplicated. It was part of the plan to account for all the available units and make sure they were in the system and removed from the system when sold or moved to other locations.

In the case of the beauty store, there were many lipsticks and other products that were unfit for sale but were still on the shelves. They all were removed and replaced by new ones.

Image 47 – Before 5S

Image 48 – After 5S

During this first stage, the stores were divided into sections with clear owners to ensure everyone knew their responsibilities.

2S – Store

Big screens were mixed with cellphones, watches, and blow driers in the home appliances store. Everything was all over the place. There were no clear rules to accommodate the articles. The owner was the one bringing the items and placing them where there was an empty spot. The more, the merrier. But this strategy was confusing for the employees. The system would show stock of an article, but they would spend several minutes looking for it.

Items were organized based on the category so that all the fridges, for example, could be found in one place. That would make it easier for the employees to show different products and reduce wasted time. Nobody, not even the owner, could change the layout unless there was a 5S reason communicated accordingly.

3S – Shine

The beauty salon had to be sparkling clean, so shine was all about defining the best ways to clean the salon and avoid getting dirty with the makeup. Transparent plastic containers were used to organize the items prone to leak. Cleaning kits were located in all the stores, especially in the bathrooms.

Customers did not usually use bathrooms, so they were not well-maintained in some of the stores. I reminded the store owners that every part of the store, no matter if it was visible or not to the client, was vital to provide the best experience. For example, if the restroom was out of order due to poor maintenance, they had to close the store for some time. Cleaning was a matter of beauty and safety and a means to detect potential problems.

4S – Standardize

In all stores, visual management was applied to ensure the system was sustained through time by posting laminated pictures on the wall or painting the shade on the floor.

5S was applied in the visible part of the store and the offices and storage locations. A small room was used as a break room, but it contained tons of folders, chairs, old equipment, and other items. It was so packed that people could barely use it. As part of the action plan of the owner of that section, the room was completely remodeled. The table and chairs were replaced, the documents stored or trashed and the board cleaned up. After the change, the room became a common area to meet, discuss ideas, or share lunch. It changed the employee's mood and became a spot for sharing and ideation (a.k.a. idea creation).

Image 49

Image 50 - Before

Image 51 - After

5S – Self-organize

All the employees were trained to guide all the self-organization efforts. The trainers scheduled quarterly audits to identify the primary sources of barriers and repetitive issues and eliminate them. Especially in the cloth apparel store, we organized coaching sessions with the store team leaders and the operations manager to analyze the audit results, remove obstacles and prioritize actions.

Different internal communication methods were established to help everyone sustain the effort, primarily visual signs and mobile apps like Whatsapp were used as employees didn't have access to computers.

5S in Healthcare and social work activities

As mentioned in the first chapter, most of the hospital errors take place in the operation room (OR)

Distractions and interruptions in the operational flow are contributing factors to medical error.

Hospital operating rooms typically generate the highest returns of all departments, yet they experience the highest costs and less available capacity. By introducing the 5S methodology, employees can decrease the turnaround time between surgical cases.

Montgomery Regional Hospital[37] , with 60 employees working at the operating room department, handled over 6,500 surgical and endoscopy cases per year across six Operating Rooms and two Endoscopy Rooms. They were operating at approximately 70% capacity, and considering that some operating rooms were reporting a cost of 10-30$ per minute

The impact of 5S

Montogomery employees implemented the 5S methodology to improve efficiency and allow more patients to be operated in the same facilities.

The turnaround time was defined as "close-to-cut," or the time from a surgeon closing the incision on Patient 1 to the same surgeon placing the cut on Patient 2.

Simple changes in how people behave turned into significant cost reductions, reduced near misses and accidents, and fewer errors in the long term. 5s reduced inventory, created space, reduced travel and search times, and, therefore, reduced errors.

---

[37]
https://www.researchgate.net/publication/237118519_Case_Study_on_Using_Lean_Principles_to_Improve_Turnaround_Time_and_First_Case_Starts_in_an_Operating_Room

---

1S - Sort

Inventory management is a critical issue in hospitals. Running out of medicine or having too many can put someone at risk or utilize much more space than needed. Removing expired and broken items can increase safety by decreasing the chance of using incorrect items for patient care.

Clear identification of areas, items and amounts can make it easier and more cost-effective to keep the inventory at the right level before and after every operation.

The first step in a 5S implementation is to remove all the unneeded items in the OR. Unfortunately, some cannot be removed, so they need to be red-tagged.

2S - Store

If items are out of place, they may cause a delay during an operation that can become very risky or life-threatening for a patient. Maybe commonly needed items are always in the same place, but that doesn't mean it is right. The right home has to be defined by everybody that is using the item, considering the weight (heavy objects should not be stored on high shelves), the size, the distance from the place where it is going to be used, the frequency of use and the effort needed to get to the object. Every minute counts in this industry, so if finding an item takes more than 30 seconds, it is probably not in the right place.

A floor plan can draw where to locate the equipment and supplies.

The Montgomery team created a standard list of items to keep in each OR. In addition, they ordered items such as rolling carts to organize items better. Commonly, these carts were overstocked due to personnel's belief that they would run out of the needed supplies.

3S - Shine

In a healthcare setting, the lack of cleanliness is a critical issue. It may cause cross-contamination, risk of trips and falls, patient dissatisfaction, and difficulty following protocols. Therefore, cleaning the OR from the previous procedure was one of the steps to be reviewed to improve the turnaround time (close-to-cut). In addition, the specific material of the floors, walls, and corners of the ORs makes it easier to clean and spot hidden sources of dirt.

It is also part of the shining stage to clean and rearrange equipment and electrical cords.

4S - Standardize

Equipment maintenance is also crucial. Having equipment out of order may be a reason for canceling appointments or increasing waiting time. The fourth step of the 5S, standardize, helps to schedule preventive maintenance routines, define standards and easily visualize any malfunctions ahead of time.

In the neurosurgery OR[38] mentioned in the first chate, all needed equipment and supplies locations were color-coded and labeled. Pictures were taken and laminated behind each piece to identify when it was missing immediately. The team developed Before Start of Day and End of Day checklists to review daily, including cleaning, restocking, and returning. They also created an OR foot traffic policy to define how to communicate equipment needs.

5S – Self-organize

The Montgomery team Created a structured audit process to monitor and sustain the 5S system of the organization.

In the case of the neurosurgery OR, the team studied the impact of 5S intervention on the craniotomy infection rates. Using control charts, they could show that there was an infection rate of 2,6 per 100 procedures by the third quarter, which is below the national benchmark. However, they also noted obstacles in implementing future projects, such as the poor maintenance of surgical equipment and, therefore, the need to implement preventive maintenance (TPM could be applied in the future).

Significant benefits in the operating room

---

[38] "The Application of the Toyota Production system Lean Lean 5S Methodology in the Operating Room Setting". Treasa "Susie" Leamng-Lee and Shea Polancich. Vanderbilt University School of Nursing https://doi.org/10.1016/j.cnur.2018.10.008

As per the Montgomery case study, the benefits of applying 5S represented significant cost reductions and an increased amount of operations. Below are mentioned some of the significant accomplishments:

- Removed equipment and carts from visible hallway space
- Reduced total inventory by about $22,000
- Reduced physical "footprint" of floor space required in the OR for equipment, instruments, and supplies by 38%
- Improved accuracy and feasibility of inventory levels
- Improved layout and flow of the case picking area

The neurosurgery results show:
- Reduced inventory by 68%, reducing costs from $460,530 to $147,363
- Increased space, due to inventory reduction two large inventory carts were removed
- Reduced waste, motion, visual confusion and distractions
- Satisfactory results convinced management to use the tools also in other supply rooms

5S improved costs and improved patient clinical outcomes, enhanced care, provided more satisfaction, reduced errors, reduced employee turnover, and increased productivity.

5s in Education
Daycares teach 5S to babies since they are very young, even without knowing it. Teachers remind kids to store everything in its place before starting the next game. They use one toy, they store it. Read the following examples from a daycare and a school.
1S – Sort
When working with babies or having babies at home, sorting is crucial to avoid accidents. You need to remove any objects that may impact their health from the room, as you cannot control every second of the life of the ten kids. Pens, small things, toys not being used, broken toys are all objects that should be removed from their sight, mainly because they get distracted easily.
2S – Store
The picture below shows how storing for ease of use is not only a matter of cleanliness but a matter of safety. Imagine you need to change diapers for ten kids, one after another. Each has different allergies or

brand preferences; it must be challenging to remember all the details. What if you are absent one day and someones else need to do it? Can you take the risk of not changing the diapers at all or making any mistakes in choosing how to do it?

Let's say you have it all organized, but when you are changing the diapers, you realize you run out of diapers. What do you do? If you leave the baby on a table for two seconds, it is almost 99% positive the baby will fall off the table. Having a visual inventory of the items needed, with labels for each baby, helps everyone know what is required, by whom and when. It's easy to see when you need to contact the mom for more diapers.

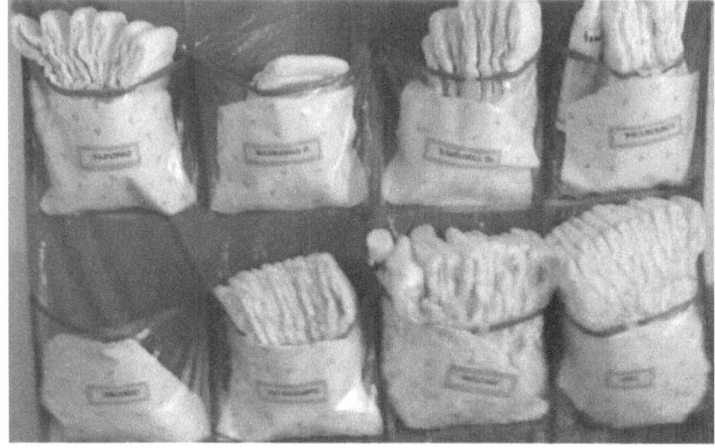

Image 52

3S – Shine

Montessori and Acton Academy schools use 5S, too, without even knowing it. They all make the children clean after themselves. They clean after lunch, using a table or playing, and clean before leaving the studio. Their responsibilities for maintenance are clear: the students are the owners of the place, not the teachers.

4S – Standardize

Standardizing is always possible and convenient, especially with kids. How do you standardize when kids cannot read labels or understand procedures? Simple. Make the rules visible and available to them. If you want them to learn where to store their backpack, identify the "home" with their picture. You can also specify the location with the image of the item. Make it a game. It doesn't have to be perfect, but it must be simple.

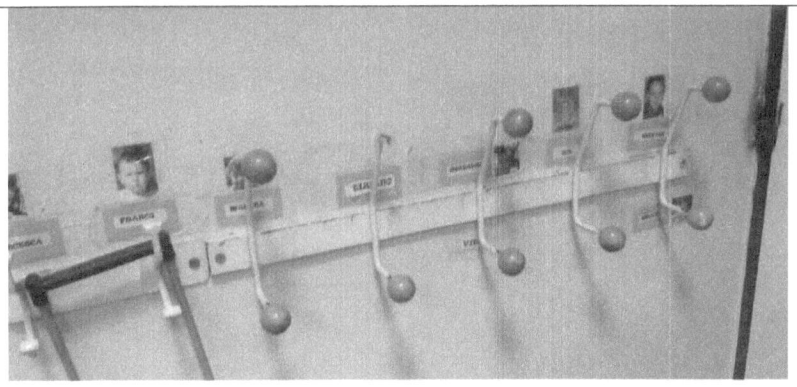

Image 53

5S – Self-organize

My daughter goes to a self-organized school too, where teachers only facilitate work, and students can advance homework on their own or slow down the pace if they need to.

During the "stay at home" due to COVID-19, her school could continue the classes almost as usual, only that the classes were remote. Students already knew how to plan, focus, and manage their time. They didn't have to wait for the teacher to send homework. They already knew the work that was in their pipeline.

The teachers organized three meetings a day to keep the CONNECTION, talk bout stories and ASK questions. Teachers RESPECTED each student's pace and EMPOWERED them to advance their studies remotely. Students just needed to decide how and when to do it. I remember teachers always talked about the "rules of engagement" during a conversation. Those are the values of self-organization. 5S builds the perfect environment to self-organize everywhere you go.

As you can see, the specific actions may vary depending on the type of the industry, but the steps and microsteps remain valid, even applying it at home.

ACKNOWLEDGMENTS

Many people contributed to the creation of this book. I wanted to start by thanking the multiple company owners, managers and employees that trusted my team and me to implement 5S. I am so proud of all that they have achieved through 5S. Hundreds of employees fueled their passion at work and strengthened their self-organization muscle.

Thanks to all the teachers, professors and experts that turned me into a 5S fan.

I owe special thanks to the contributions of friends and professionals who read the drafts of the manuscript to help me improve along the way. Jessica Fant helped me transform the chapters by making them more visual, interactive and straightforward. Peter Merril, as an innovator, helped me think out of the box and re-design the cover, title, content and the introduction of the book. Mohammad Hossein Zavvar Sabegh contributed with research documents to support the tool's benefits and the case studies. I am also grateful to Austin Lin for writing such an excellent foreword.

The SSI team helped develop the platform "The We Culture" that complements this book. Download it to your phone or computer to capture your improvements in an action plan, watch 5S videos or learn about other productivity tools.

Lastly, I wanted to thank my family for supporting me in writing this book during the pandemic. In particular, my husband Guillermo Maiale, my daughter Sol, my mother Beatriz Dubischar, my father Mario Paulise and my brother Alexis Paulise. Also, my friends have supported me so much, especially Pilar Milano. Thank you for supporting me. Challenging times make us stronger.

ABOUT THE AUTHOR

PHOTO: kimberlydianne.com

Luciana Paulise (a.k.a Lu) is a culture coach, speaker and author. She is MBA, Quality Engineer, Certified Scrum Master and Agile Coach. As an accomplished book author, Luciana has contributed to multiple international media outlets such as ThriveGlobal.com, Quality Progress and is currently a Forbes Contributor. Lu has helped a wide range of companies, from small businesses to Fortune 100 companies, transform their employee's culture to become more agile, engaged and innovative. She is the CEO of Biztorming Training & Consulting LLC. Luciana is also ASQ West South-Central Regional Deputy Director and has served for various non-profits as chair and advisor, and was the co-founder of the SETX Hispanic Women's Network. She is bilingual English-Spanish.

Thank you for purchasing this book. I am sure it will help you and your team get more productive, organized and happy. Remember, it is not just about you; you can help to build an environment where enjoying and being productive is possible.

What do you think? I want to hear from you! Your thoughts and comments are important to me. If you enjoyed this book or found it useful, post a short review on Amazon or message me. Thanks again for your support!

Luciana Paulise
luciana@biztorming.com
@lupaulise

Lu Paulise

Visit
www.biztorming.com
To learn about our Training and consulting services to assist you in implementing 5S

Visit
www.theweculture.com
To learn about more online tools and courses to improve your 5S experience, download your action plan and access other resources to continue your self-improvement journey. Use the QR code below to download the app.